WORD

TO LIVE BY

A
PIECE
OF
PEACE

SHAROQ ALMALKI

ISBN-13: 978-1500752262
ISBN-10: 1500752266
LCCN: 2014914085
BISAC: Business & Economics / Personal Success

Mom and Dad, what you've both taught
me can't be expressed in words...

CONTENTS

Introduction 9

Story #1: Thirsty for Knowledge 10

Story #2: A Fish "Tail" 12

Story #3: The Difference Between Heaven and Hell. . . 14

Story #4: Just One Move. 16

Story #5: The Invoice 18

Story #6: Keep Believing in Yourself 20

Story #7: The Office Boy 22

Story #8: Vanilla or Chocolate? 24

Story #9: Spilled Milk. 26

Story #10: The Elephant Trainer 28

Story #11: The Pencil Maker 30

Story #12: Father and Daughter 32

Story #13: The Emperor and the Seeds 34

Story #14: The Empty Soap Boxes 36

Story #15: Biscuits 38

Story #16: Fly Like an Eagle. 40

Story #17: The Scratch. 42

Story #18: The Funeral. 44

Story #19: The Penny. 45

Story #20: Starfish 46

Story #21: Feeding Your Wolves 47

Story #22: The Bus Station. 48

Story #23: The King and the Consultant. 49

Story #24: In Hot Water. 50

Story #25: Heads or Tails. 52

Story #26: An Even Playing Field. 54

Story #27: The Turtle 56

Story #28: You (Almost) Sank My Battleship! 57

Story #29: The Bank President. 58

Story #30: Out of Service. 59

Story #31: The Obituary. 60

Story #32: Bird's Eye 61

Story #33: Socrates and the Secret of Success 62

Story #34: The Frog and the Pit 64

Story #35: The Woodcutter and His Ax 66

Story #36: The Disciple and His Teacher. 68

Story #37: The Graduate 70

Story #38: The Wise Advisor and His Students. 71

Story #39: The Ark's Rules. 72

Story #40: The Three Stonecutters 74

Story #41: This Too Shall Pass 76

Story #42: The Lions and the Gazelles 77

Story #43: Efficiency Versus Effectiveness. 78

Story #44: Backseat Drivers 79

Story #45: The Farmer and the Professors 80

Story #46: The Million-Dollar Lesson. 81

Story #47: Not Enough Chickens. 82

Story #48: The Sleeping Farmhand 83

Story #49: The CEO and the Banana. 84

Story #50: The Salesmen 85

Story #51: The Surgeon and the Mechanic. 86

Story #52: The Price of Expectations 87

Story #53: The Durian Tree 88

Story #54: The Violin Lesson 89

Story #55: The Teacup. 90

Story #56: The Haircut 91

Story #57: The Littlest Wave 92

Story #58: The Fly and the Ant 93

Story #59: The Detour 94

Story #60: The Warrior 96

Story #61: The Violinist 97

Story #62: The Exam 98

Story #63: The Vacuum Salesman 99

Story #64: The Pedicure 100

Story #65: The King and the Wise Man 101

Story #66: The Holiday 102

Story #67: The Artists 103

Story #68: The Interview 104

Story #69: The Bus Stop 105

Story #70: The Rock Formation 106

Story #71: The Salesmen 107

Story #72: The Art Collection 108

Story #73: The Prayer 109

Story #74: The Psychiatrist 110

Story #75: The Musician and the Maid 111

Story #76: The Sports Car and the Jalopy 112

Story #77: Two Fortune Cookies 113

Story #78: The Tip 114

Story #79: Two Gardens 115

Story #80: The Hummingbird and the Snail 116

Story #81: The Confession 117

Story #82: The Painting 118

Story #83: The Cashier 119

Story #84: The Pebble, the Rock, and the Boulder 120

Story #85: Two Squirrels 121

Story #86: The Leaf and the Branch 122

Story #87: The Key. 124

Story #88: The Apple, the Banana, and the Nut. 125

Story #89: The Foxhole 126

Story #90: The Interpreter 127

Story #91: The Unemployed 128

Story #92: The Raccoon and the Cat. 130

Story #93: The Duel 131

Story #94: The Receipt. 132

Story #95: The Mosquito and the Bee 133

Story #96: The Obituary. 134

Story #97: The Snake in the Grass. 135

Story #98: The Nurse and Her Patient. 136

Story #99: The Singer. 137

Story #100: The Red Carpet 138

Story #101: The Hoarder 139

Story #102: The Runner and the Walker 140

Story #103: The Novelist 141

Story #104: The Janitor 142

Story #105: The Doctor and His Patient 143

Story #106: The Chef and the Child 144

Story #107: The Lion Tamer. 145

Story #108: The Snow and the Rain 146

Story #109: The Usher 147

Story #110: The Monk and the Tourist 148

Conclusion 149

INTRODUCTION

The quest for wisdom is an ageless pursuit, and if you are reading this, I applaud you for seeking higher learning. I too am a life-long learner, and have been collecting fables, stories, anecdotes, allegories, and little kernels and nuggets of fancy for years and sharing them with students, friends, family, colleagues, and anyone who will listen.

Now it is your turn.

Wisdom is eternal, it seems, and can be found in the stories of earliest man. And so it is that the one hundred and ten stories presented here run the gamut from ancient times and Socrates to modern topics like sports cars and cell phones.

Just as from ancient times, there is insight to be found in tales from modern times. Hopefully the variety of these stories in length, content, style, humor, grace, and ultimately knowledge will provide wisdom at every turn.

While some of the stories are about work, many center on other areas of life such as family and community. Read them to discover how you can be a more efficient, wise, energetic, knowledgeable, and above all, compassionate worker regardless of the size of your company or your role in it. We all have roles to play. It is my hope that these stories will not only help you find your role, but embrace it as you move forward through your journey to personal and professional wisdom.

THIRSTY FOR KNOWLEDGE

One day, a professor began his class by holding up a glass with some water in it. He then asked the students, "How much do you think this glass weighs?"

The students, curious, began calling out answers.

"Fifty grams!"

"One hundred grams!"

"A hundred and twenty-five grams!"

With a curious grin, the professor said, "I really don't know unless I weigh it. But my question is: What would happen if I held it up like this for a few minutes?"

A few of the students mumbled until one answered, "Nothing."

The professor nodded. "OK, then. What would happen if I held it up like this for an hour?"

"That's easy," said one of the students. "Your arm would begin to ache."

The professor nodded. "You're right. Now what would happen if I held it for a day?"

"Your arm could go numb," ventured another student. "You might have severe muscle stress and paralysis, and you'd have to go to the hospital for sure!"

Several students and even the professor laughed.

"Very good, but during all this, did the weight of the glass change?" asked the professor.

After a brief pause, the class murmured a unanimous "no."

The professor stared at them. "Then what caused the arm ache and the muscle stress?"

The students were puzzled.

"Or let me put it this way. What should I do now to come out of the pain?"

"Put the glass down!" said one of the students.

"Exactly!" said the professor.

The Moral of the Story

Life's problems are often quite similar to the glass of water in this story: Hold on to them for a few minutes in your head, and they seem OK. Dwell on them for much longer, and your head begins to ache. Become preoccupied with them to the exclusion of almost everything else, and they paralyze you. You won't be able to do anything.

It's important to think of the challenges or problems in your life, but even more important is to put them down at the end of every day before you go to sleep. That way you are not stressed; you wake up every day fresh and strong and can handle any issue and any challenge that comes your way!

A FISH "TAIL"

The Japanese have always loved fresh fish. But the waters close to Japan have not held many fish for decades. So to feed the Japanese population, fishing boats got bigger and went farther than ever to catch their precious cargo. The farther the fishermen went, however, the longer it took to bring in the fish. If the return trip took more than a few days, the fish were no longer fresh.

The Japanese did not like the taste of days-old fish. To solve this problem, fishing companies installed freezers on their boats. That way they could catch the fish and freeze them at sea. Freezers allowed the boats to go farther to catch fish and stay there longer. However, the Japanese could taste the difference between fresh and frozen, and they simply did not like frozen fish. As a result the frozen fish brought lower prices.

So fishing companies improvised again: They installed fish tanks. They would catch the fish and stuff them in the tanks fin to fin. After a little thrashing around, the fish would stop moving. They'd be tired and dull but alive.

Unfortunately the Japanese could still taste the difference. Because the fish did not move for days, they lost their fresh-fish taste. The Japanese preferred the lively taste of fresh fish, not sluggish fish.

So how did Japanese fishing companies solve this problem? How do they get fresh-tasting fish to Japan? They still put the fish in the tanks. But now they add a small shark to each tank. The shark eats a few fish, but most of the others arrive in a very lively state.

The Moral of the Story

Like the fish in this story, we are kept fresh by challenges. They may not seem pleasant at the time, and we may even feel like they are interrupting our carefully planned journeys. But without detours, obstacles, and challenges, we might become complacent and lose our freshness.

Therefore let life's challenges work *for* you, not *against* you.

THE DIFFERENCE BETWEEN HEAVEN AND HELL

A king was having a conversation with a wise man one day and said, "Wise man, I would like to know what heaven and hell are like."

The wise man led the king to two doors. He opened one and the king looked inside. In the middle of the room was a large, round table. In the middle of the table was a large pot of stew that smelled delicious and made the king's mouth water.

Even so, the people sitting around the table were thin and sickly. They appeared to be famished, on the verge of starving to death. They were holding spoons with very long handles, which made it possible to reach into the pot of stew and take a spoonful, but because the handles were longer than their arms they could not get them back into their mouths. The king shuddered at the sight of their misery and suffering.

"You have just seen hell," said the wise man, shutting the door to the first room. "Now let us see heaven."

They went to the next room and opened the door. It was exactly the same as the first one. There was the large, round table with the large pot of stew that once again made the king's mouth water with its rich, savory scent. The people were equipped with the same long-handled spoons, but here the people were well nourished and plump, laughing and talking.

The king said, "I don't understand!"

"It is simple," said the wise man. "It requires only one skill. You see, the long-handled spoon doesn't allow them to reach their mouths, so each one feeds the person facing him across the table instead of trying to feed himself. In this way the people in this room have learned to feed each other, while the greedy souls in the first room think only of themselves.

The Moral of the Story

Once we realize that teamwork is the difference between heaven and hell, it all seems so easy. But many of us would often rather starve than ask for help. We feel this may mark us as weak or inferior and hence try to solve every situation ourselves regardless of the skills and talents of our team members. Success and happiness are both about effective teamwork, so we must work as a team to make the workplace something special.

JUST ONE MOVE

Despite the fact that he had lost his left arm in a devastating car accident, a ten-year-old boy decided to study judo. He took lessons with an old Japanese judo master. The boy was doing well, so he couldn't understand why, after three months of training, the master had taught him only one move.

"Sensei," the boy finally said, "shouldn't I be learning more moves?"

"This is the only move you know, but this is the only move you'll ever need to know," the sensei replied, disappointing the boy again.

Not quite understanding but believing in his teacher, the boy kept training. Several months later the sensei took him to his first tournament.

Surprising himself, the boy easily won his first two matches. The third match proved to be more difficult, but after some time his opponent became impatient and charged; the boy deftly used his one move to win the match. Still amazed by his success, the boy now found himself in the finals.

This time his opponent was bigger, stronger, and more experienced than him. For a while the boy appeared to be overmatched. Concerned that he might get hurt, the referee called a time-out.

He was about to stop the match when the sensei intervened.

"No," the sensei insisted. "Let him continue."

Soon after the match resumed, the boy's opponent made a critical mistake: He dropped his guard. Instantly the boy used his move to pin him. The boy had won the match and the tournament for his weight category. He was the champion!

On the way home, the boy and his sensei reviewed every move in each and every match. Then the boy summoned the courage to ask what was really on his mind.

"Sensei, how did I win the tournament and become champion with only one move?"

"You won for two reasons," the sensei answered. "First, you've almost mastered one of the most difficult throws in all of judo. And second, the only known defense for that move is for your opponent to grab your left arm."

Suddenly it occurred to him: The boy's biggest weakness had become his biggest strength.

The Moral of the Story

We often blame God, circumstances, or even ourselves for what we perceive as our biggest weaknesses. Unfortunately we never give ourselves time to think about how to use them and turn them into our unique strengths.

Life is within our hands; we design our own successes and even our own failures. When viewed in the right perspective, we are surrounded by all the tools, factors, and equipment we need to succeed. We just need to understand how to use them to continue our journey.

THE INVOICE

There once was a mighty ship whose engine had failed. The ship's owners summoned one expert after another, but none of them could figure out how to fix the engine. Then, on the recommendation of some friends, they brought in an old man who had been fixing ships since he was a youngster. He carried a large bag of tools that he could hardly manage. When he arrived he immediately went to work. He inspected the engine very carefully top to bottom. Two of the ship's owners were there watching this man, hoping he would know what to do.

After looking things over, the old man reached into his bag and pulled out a small hammer. He gently tapped a small piece close to the engine. Instantly the engine lurched to life. He carefully put his hammer away. The engine was fixed!

A week later the owners received a bill from the old man for $10,000.

"What?" one of them exclaimed. "He hardly did anything!"

So they wrote the old man a note: "Please send us an itemized bill!"

The man sent back a bill that read as follows:

Tapping with a hammer = $2.
Knowing where to tap = $9,998.

The Moral of the Story

Effort is important. However, never forget that knowing where to make an effort in life makes all the difference. We have been taught that if we work hard, we'll succeed, but working hard is no longer a guarantee of success.

Modern success—the kind our increasingly complex, sophisticated, and technological world requires—is not driven just by how *hard* we work but by how *smart* we work.

Story #6

KEEP BELIEVING IN YOURSELF

A professor stood before his class of thirty senior molecular biology students, about to pass out the final exam.

"I have been privileged to be your instructor this semester," he stated, "and I know how hard you have all worked to prepare for today's exam. I also know most of you are off to medical school next fall. I am well aware of how much pressure you are under to keep your GPAs up, and because I know you are all capable of understanding this material, I am prepared to offer an automatic B to anyone who would prefer not to take the final."

The relief was audible as a number of students jumped up to thank the professor and departed from class.

The professor looked at the handful of students who remained and said, "Any other takers, gang? This is your last opportunity."

Two more students looked at each other, thought about it carefully, and decided to go.

After the exodus, seven students remained. The professor closed the door and took attendance. He unsealed his envelope, looked into the face of each student, and handed out the final exams.

"Please keep the exam papers face down on the table until I say it's time to turn them over," he warned the students. Dutifully they obeyed. When all the tests had been handed out, the professor returned to his podium, looked at his stopwatch, and announced, "You have fifteen minutes to hand back your answers. Please proceed with the questions."

The students turn over the exam papers and found two sentences typed on the front of each: "Congratulations. You have just received an A in this class. Keep believing in yourself."

The Moral of the Story

Imagine these seven students' surprise when they saw that message printed on the exams. Imagine their relief! But the message is so true: Success does lie in believing in yourself, because only you can define your measures of success. Those around you also have much to contribute and they deserve your support. Without faith in yourself and others, success is impossible.

Psychologists say that by the age of two, fifty percent of what we believe about ourselves has already been formed; by age six it's sixty percent, and at eight years eighty percent of what we will believe to be true about ourselves has already been deeply ingrained in our psyches. Wouldn't you love to have the energy and optimism of a little kid? There would be nothing you couldn't do or learn or be.

However, you're a big kid now, and you realize you have some limits. Don't let the biggest limit be yourself. Take your cue from Sir Edmund Hillary, the first person to reach the summit of Mount Everest, who said, "It's not the mountain we conquer but ourselves."

Story #7

THE OFFICE BOY

A jobless man applied for the position of office boy at a very big firm. The HR manager who interviewed him gave him a simple test: Clean the floor.

"You are hired," she said, upon admiring the spotless floor. "Now, give me your e-mail address, and I'll send you the application to fill out as well as the date when you will start."

The man replied, "I don't have a computer or an e-mail account."

"I'm sorry," said the HR manager. "If you don't have an e-mail address, that means you do not exist. And if you don't exist, how can you have the job?"

The man left with no hope at all and with only ten dollars in his pocket. He didn't know what to do. Passing a supermarket on his way home, he decided to go in and spend his last ten dollars to buy a crate of tomatoes.

He then went around the block selling the tomatoes door to door. In less than two hours, he succeeded in doubling his capital. He repeated the operation until his feet were sore and it was getting dark, and he returned home with sixty dollars.

The man realized he could survive very easily this way and went out on his rounds earlier every day and returned later. Thus his money doubled or tripled every day. A short time later, he bought a cart and then a truck, and before long he had his own fleet of vegetable-delivery vehicles.

Five years later the man had become one of the biggest food retailers in the United States. He started to plan his family's future and decided to buy a life insurance policy. He called an insurance broker and chose a protection plan. When the conversation was concluded, the broker asked him his e-mail address.

The man replied, "I'm sorry; I don't have an e-mail account."

The broker replied, "I'm amazed. You've succeeded in building an empire. Do you imagine what you could have been if you had e-mail?"

The man thought about it, and replied, "An office boy!"

The Moral of the Story

While technology has certainly been a blessing for a variety of reasons, we often emphasize the tools we use, with the result that we kill the motivators inside us that drive our creativity.

It has been reported that historically, even ordinary people were able to memorize a full speech and more than one hundred lines of poetry from listening to them just once or twice. Nowadays, however, we are barely able to recall the names of ten new people who attend a meeting with us. It's not that we're less smart, exactly; we have simply become dependent on technology. After all, if we forget someone's name, we can always go back to retrieve the information in our phones, our e-mail, and so on. But as we do so, we are killing our abilities and capabilities. Don't let technology and tools drive you; drive them instead. Use them to manage your time instead of letting them manage you.

Story #8

VANILLA OR CHOCOLATE?

The Pontiac division of General Motors once received the following complaint:

> This is the second time I have written to you, and I don't blame you for not answering me, because I know this sounds crazy, but we have a tradition in our family of serving ice cream for dessert after dinner each night. However, the kind of ice cream varies, so every night, after we've eaten, the whole family votes on which flavor of ice cream we should have, either chocolate or vanilla, and I drive down to the store to get it.
>
> I recently purchased a new Pontiac and since then my trips to the store have created a problem. You see, every time I buy vanilla ice cream, when I start back from the store, my car won't start. If I get chocolate, the car starts just fine. I want you to know I'm serious about this question, no matter how silly it sounds: What is it about a Pontiac that makes it not start when I get vanilla ice cream and easy to start whenever I get chocolate ice cream?

While the president of Pontiac was understandably skeptical about the letter, he sent an engineer to check out the problem anyway. The engineer arranged to meet the man who had written the letter just after dinnertime, and the two hopped into the car and drove to the local ice cream store. It was vanilla ice cream that night, and sure enough, after they came back to the car it wouldn't start.

The engineer returned for three more nights. The first night they got chocolate. The car started. The second night they got chocolate again, and the car started. The third night the man ordered vanilla. The car failed to start, and it kept refusing to start whenever they bought vanilla. Could the letter writer be right? It certainly sounded like his car was allergic to vanilla ice cream!

Now the engineer, being a logical man, refused to believe that. Therefore he arranged to continue his visits for as long as it took to solve the problem. And toward this end, he took notes. He jotted down all sorts of data: time of day, type of gas used, time to drive back and forth, and so on.

After some time he had a clue: The man took less time to buy vanilla than chocolate. Why? The answer was in the layout of the store. Vanilla, being the most popular flavor, was in a separate case at the front of the store for quick pickup. All the other flavors, including chocolate, were kept in the back of the store, at a different counter where it took considerably longer to check out.

The engineer was getting warm! The problem was *time*, he decided, not the flavor of ice cream. The question he wanted to answer was: Why wouldn't the car start when it took less time?

The engineer quickly came up with the answer: vapor lock. Apparently the extra time it took the man to get chocolate ice cream allowed the engine to cool down sufficiently to start. When he got vanilla, the engine was still too hot for the vapor lock to dissipate. Problem solved; case closed!

The Moral of the Story

General Motors could have simply discounted this letter writer as another crackpot, and the engineer never would have realized the car's problem with vapor lock during stop-and-go starting. Instead it delved further and solved a crucial dilemma.

Whenever facing a problem in your life, never try to jump to a conclusion without giving considerable time to analyzing the situation in a proper manner.

Story #9

SPILLED MILK

A newspaper reporter was interviewing a famous research scientist who had made several very important medical breakthroughs. The reporter asked him why he thought he was able to be so much more creative than the average person.

"What sets you far apart from others?"

The scientist responded that in his opinion, it all came from an experience with his mother that had occurred when he was about two years old. He had been trying to remove a bottle of milk from the refrigerator when he lost his grip on the slippery bottle and it fell, spilling its contents all over the kitchen floor—a veritable sea of milk!

When his mother came into the kitchen, instead of yelling at him, giving him a lecture, or punishing him, she said, "Robert, what a great and wonderful mess you have made! I have rarely seen such a huge puddle of milk. Well, the damage has already been done. Would you like to get down and play in the milk for a few minutes before we clean it up?"

Indeed he did. After a few minutes, his mother said, "You know, Robert, whenever you make a mess like this, eventually you have to clean it up and restore everything to its proper order. So how would you like to do that? We could use a sponge, a towel, or a mop. Which do you prefer?"

He chose the sponge, and together they cleaned up the spilled milk.

His mother then said, "You know, what we have here is a failed experiment in how to carry a big milk bottle effectively with two tiny hands. Let's go out in the backyard and fill the bottle with water and see if you can discover a way to carry it without dropping it."

The little boy learned that if he grasped the bottle at the top near the lip with both hands, he could carry it without dropping it. What a wonderful lesson!

This renowned scientist then remarked that it was at that very moment that he knew he didn't need to be afraid to make mistakes.

Instead he learned that mistakes are just opportunities for learning new things, which is, after all, what scientific experiments are all about. Even if the experiment doesn't work, we usually learn something valuable from it.

The Moral of the Story

We often worry about making mistakes, even driving ourselves to distraction in our efforts to be perfect. Yet clearly a mistake is simply the discovery of a way that does not work.

Mistakes are, in fact, signs that there are other ways to approach problems; they represent, as we say, the "trial and error" approach. But we can't learn from our mistakes if we don't make any. So don't be afraid: Make all the mistakes you want and grow smarter every day!

THE ELEPHANT TRAINER

As a person from the city was walking past some elephants, he suddenly stopped, confused by the fact that these huge creatures were being held by only slender ropes tied to their front legs. No chains, no cages. It was obvious that the elephants could at any time break free of the ropes, but for some reason they did not. That person saw a trainer nearby and asked why these beautiful, magnificent animals just stood there and made no attempt to get away.

"Well," said the trainer, "when they are very young and much smaller, we use the same sized ropes to tie them, and at that age it's enough to hold them. As they grow up, they are conditioned to believe they cannot break away. They believe the ropes can still hold them, so they never try to break free."

The person was amazed. These animals could at any time break free from their bonds, but because they believed they couldn't, they were stuck right where they were.

The Moral of the Story

Like the elephants in this fable, how many of us go through life hanging on to beliefs that we cannot do something simply because we failed at it once before? And why shouldn't we try it again?

Your attempt may fail, but never fail to make an attempt! Never accept the false boundaries and limitations created by the past. If you want something you never had, do something you have never done before.

Don't go the way life takes you; take life the way you want to go.

Remember that you are born to live, not living simply because you were born.

THE PENCIL MAKER

There once lived a wise pencil maker. He had the amazing ability to converse with pencils. One day, just before putting one into the box for delivery, he took it aside.

"There are five things you need to know before I send you out into the world," the pencil maker told the pencil. "Always remember them, and never forget, and you will become the best pencil you can be.

"First, you will be able to do many great things but only if you allow yourself to be held in someone's hand.

"Second, you will experience a painful sharpening from time to time, but you will need it to become a better pencil.

"Third, you will be able to correct any mistakes you might make.

"Fourth, the most important part of you will always be what's inside.

"And finally, little pencil, you must leave your mark on every surface on which you are used. No matter what the condition, you must continue to write."

The pencil understood and promised to remember, and it went into the box with purpose in its heart. For that reason, pencils are so useful that most planners and designers like to use them instead of pens.

The Moral of the Story

Like the pencil, we must remember that we will be able to do many great things—but only if we allow other human beings to access the many gifts we possess and reveal the different talents that are hidden within our best selves.

FATHER AND DAUGHTER

A little girl and her father were crossing a bridge. The father was afraid, so he said to his daughter, "Sweetheart, please hold my hand so you don't fall into the river."

The little girl said, "No, Dad. *You* hold *my* hand."

"What's the difference?" asked the puzzled father.

"There's a big difference," replied the little girl. "If I hold your hand and something happens to me, chances are I may let your hand go. But if you hold my hand, I know for sure that no matter what happens, you will never let my hand go."

The Moral of the Story

The little girl's wisdom can't be underestimated, for her advice is so wise: Hold the hand of the person you lead rather than expecting him or her to hold yours. This helps us to build trust among those with whom we walk and for them to trust us as well.

THE EMPEROR AND THE SEEDS

An emperor in the Far East was growing old and knew it was time to choose his successor. He had five brilliants sons, and it was really difficult to choose one of them. Instead of choosing the eldest one, as tradition dictates, he decided to do something different.

He called his sons and said, "It is time for me to step down and choose the next emperor. I have decided to choose one of you."

His sons became anxious at the news.

The emperor continued, "I am going to give each one of you a seed today—one very special seed. I want you to plant it, water it, take care of it, and come back here one year from today with what you have grown from this one seed. I will then judge the plants you bring, and the son I choose will be the next emperor."

Ling, the youngest of his sons, was there that day and received a seed. He went home and excitedly told his wife the story. She helped him get a pot and soil, and he planted the seed. Every day he watered it and watched to see if it had grown.

After about three weeks, some of the other brothers talked about their seeds and the plants that were growing. Ling kept checking his seed, but nothing ever grew. Weeks and weeks went by—still nothing in Ling's pot. Six months went by—still nothing. He believed he had killed his seed. His brothers had trees and tall plants, but he had nothing, and he felt like a failure.

Ling didn't say anything to his brothers. He just kept waiting for his seed to grow.

After a year, all the brothers brought their plants to the emperor for inspection. Ling told his wife that he wasn't going to take an empty pot, but she said he must be honest about what had happened. Ling felt sick to his stomach, but he knew his wife was right, as it is not wise at all to run away from a failure.

He took his empty pot to the palace. When he arrived, he was amazed by the variety of plants the other brothers had grown. They were beautiful and in all shapes and sizes. Ling put his empty pot on the floor, and his brothers laughed at him. The oldest felt sorry for him and just said, "Ling, nice try."

When the emperor arrived, he surveyed the room and greeted his sons. Ling tried to hide in the back.

"My beloved sons, what great plants, trees, and flowers you have grown," said the emperor. "Today one of you will be appointed as the next emperor!"

All of a sudden, he spotted Ling at the back of the room with his empty pot. He ordered his guards to bring him to the front.

Ling was terrified. *The emperor knows I'm a failure! he thought. Maybe he'll have me killed.*

When Ling got to the front, the emperor shouted at him, "Ling, what have you been doing the entire year?"

Ling felt that death was near. All the rest were laughing and making fun of him. The emperor asked everyone to quiet down. He looked at Ling and then announced to the crowd, "Behold your new emperor! His name is Ling."

Ling couldn't believe it. He couldn't even grow his seed. How could he be the new emperor?

Then the emperor said, "One year ago today, I gave everyone here a seed. I told you to take the seed, plant it, water it, and bring it back to me today. But I gave you all boiled seeds that would not grow. All of you except Ling have brought me trees and plants and flowers. When you found that the seeds would not grow, you substituted other seeds for the ones I gave you. Ling was the only one with the honesty and courage to bring me a pot with my seed in it. Therefore he is the one who will be the new emperor."

The Moral of the Story

If you plant honesty, you will reap trust—even from boiled seeds. Admitting what may seem to you like a failure is the only true path to understanding success. Honesty brings courage with it, and courage leads to success.

THE EMPTY SOAP BOXES

One of the most memorable case studies on Japanese management was the case of the empty soap boxes, which happened in one of Japan's biggest cosmetics companies.

The company received a complaint that a few consumers had bought soap but found the boxes were empty. The authorities immediately isolated the problem to the assembly line, which transported all the packaged boxes of soap to the delivery department. The company had two different production units located in different cities. They concluded that for some reason, soap boxes went through the assembly line empty.

The management of the production unit in city A asked its engineers to solve the problem. Immediately the engineers worked hard to devise an X-ray machine with high-resolution monitors manned by two people who could watch all the soap boxes that passed through the line and make sure they were not empty. No doubt they had worked hard and fast, but they had spent and engaged many resources to do so (time, money, and two extra staff as X-ray machine operators).

On the other hand, to simplify the case, the management of the production unit in city B approached their workers to generate ideas that might solve the problem. One of the workers came up with the solution. He bought a strong, industrial electric fan and pointed it at the assembly line. He switched the fan on, and as each soap box passed the fan, it simply blew the empty boxes out of the line.

The Moral of the Story

There is always beauty in simplicity! Learn to focus on solutions, not on problems. Always look for the simplest possible solution that can solve a problem.

Also, as leaders, managers, and team members, we are asked to utilize our resources best by being open, acknowledging effort, and encouraging contributions from our people. Teamwork can achieve incredible success!

Story #15

BISCUITS

A sociologist recently interviewed a production line worker in a biscuit factory.

"How long have you worked here?" he asked.

"Since I left school," she answered. "About fifteen years."

"What do you do?"

"I take packets of biscuits off the conveyor belt and put them into cardboard boxes."

"Have you always done the same job?"

"Yes."

"Do you enjoy it?"

"Oh, my, yes," said the factory worker. "It's great. Everyone is so nice and friendly, and we have a good laugh sometimes."

With a hint of disbelief, the interviewer asked, "Really? Don't you find it a bit boring?"

"Oh no," she answered without a trace of irony. "Sometimes they change the biscuits."

The Moral of the Story

Remember that not everyone defines success the same way, so don't impose your needs and ambitions on other people who may not share them. Don't assume that things that motivate you will motivate someone else. Instead recognize that sources of happiness may vary widely and accept others for the joy they bring to the table, not what you perceive as their level of ambition.

FLY LIKE AN EAGLE

Once upon a time, an eagle's nest rested on a steep mountainside. The nest contained four large eagle eggs. One day an earthquake rocked the mountain, causing one of the eggs to roll down the mountain and into a chicken farm located in the valley bellow.

The chickens knew they needed to protect and care for the strange egg, so an old hen volunteered to nurture and raise it. One day the egg hatched and a fledgling eagle was born.

He was raised to be a chicken, and soon even he believed he was one.

Eventually, although he loved his home and family, his spirit cried out for more.

While playing a game on the farm one day, he looked to the skies above and noticed a group of mighty eagles soaring through the clouds.

"Oh!" he cried. "I wish I could soar like those birds."

The chickens roared with laughter. "You cannot soar with those birds!" they said. "You are a chicken, and chickens do not soar."

The eagle continued staring at his real family up above, dreaming that he could be with them one day. Each time he let his dreams be known, however, he was told it simply couldn't be done, and sadly that was what the eagle learned to believe. After a time he simply stopped dreaming and continued to live his life as a chicken.

Finally, after a long life as a chicken, the eagle passed away.

The Moral of the Story

You become what you believe you are, so if you ever dream of becoming an eagle, follow your dreams—and not the words of a chicken.

THE SCRATCH

A gentleman once visited a museum that was under construction. There he saw a sculptor making a statue of a martyr. Suddenly he noticed a similar statue lying nearby. Surprised, he asked the sculptor, "Do you need two statues of the same symbol?"

"No," said the sculptor without looking up. "We need only one, but the first got damaged during the last stage of carving."

The gentleman examined the statue and found no apparent marks. "Where is the damage?"

"There is a scratch on the nose," said the sculptor, still busy with his work.

"Where are you going to install the statue?" the man asked.

The sculptor replied that it would be installed on a pillar twenty feet high.

"If the statue is that far away, who is going to know there is a scratch on the nose?" the gentleman asked.

The sculptor stopped his work, looked up at the gentleman, smiled, and said, "I'd know it, and God would know it!"

The Moral of the Story

Excellence is a drive from inside, not outside. You should never be connected to what others feel about your desires for success. Excel at a task today—not for someone else to notice but for your own satisfaction.

THE FUNERAL

One day all the employees in an office went to work and saw a big sign on the door that read, "Yesterday the person who has been hindering your growth in this company passed away. We invite you to join the funeral in the room that has been prepared in the gym."

At first the employees were sad over the death of one of their colleagues, but after a while they were curious to know who had hindered the growth of his colleagues and the company itself.

The more people reached the coffin, the more the excitement heated up. Everyone wondered who this guy was who had hindered their progress. Others thought, *Well, at least he died!*

One by one the curious employees got closer to the coffin, and when each looked inside it they were speechless. There was a mirror inside the coffin, so everyone who looked in could see himself or herself. There was a sign next to the mirror that said: "There is only one person who is capable of limiting your growth: you."

The Moral of the Story

It's not what happens to you that matters the most; what makes the difference is the way you face life. Remember that you are the only person who can revolutionize your life. You are the only person who can influence your happiness, your realizations, and your success.

Your life does not change when your boss changes, when your friends change, or even when your company changes. Your life changes when *you* change and when you go beyond your limiting beliefs.

THE PENNY

One day a little child was playing with a very valuable vase. He put his hand inside but couldn't get it out. His father tried his best to free his son's hand, but his efforts were in vain.

The family was thinking of breaking the very expensive vase when the father said, "Now, my son, make one more try. Open your hand, and hold your fingers out straight as you see me doing, and then pull."

To their astonishment the little fellow said, "Oh no, father. I couldn't put my fingers out like that because if I did, I would drop my penny."

The Moral of the Story

We are often like that little boy: so busy holding on to a single penny that we cannot accept liberation. Now is the time to drop unnecessary worries from your path and build up your destiny the way you want it. With joy in your heart and a relaxed mind, recognize that the future is in your hands.

STARFISH

There was once a wise man who went to the ocean to do his writing. He had a habit of walking on the beach before he began his work. One day as he was walking, he looked down the beach and saw a human figure moving like a dancer. He smiled, thinking it was someone who would dance to greet the day. He walked faster to catch up.

As he got closer, he saw that it was a young man, and the young man wasn't dancing but reaching down to the sand, picking up something, and very gently throwing it into the ocean.

When the wise man got closer, he called out, "Good morning! What are you doing?"

The young man paused, looked up, and replied, "Throwing starfish in the ocean."

"Why are you throwing starfish in the ocean?"

"The sun is up, and the tide is going out, and if I don't throw them in they'll die."

The wise man looked along the coastline, shaking his head. "But young man, don't you realize there are miles and miles of beach, and starfish all along it? You can't possibly make a difference."

The young man listened politely. Then he bent down, picked up another starfish, and threw it into the sea, past the breaking waves. He said, "It made a difference for that one."

The Moral of the Story

There is something very special in each and every one of us. Each of us has been given the ability to make a difference; it is our responsibility to become aware of that gift and use it wisely.

FEEDING YOUR WOLVES

One day, an old man's grandson came to him, angry at a school-mate who had done him an injustice.

The grandfather sat the boy down and said, "Let me tell you a story. At times I have also felt a great hate for those who have taken so much from me with no sorrow for what they do. However, hate wears you down and does not hurt your enemy. It is like taking poison and wishing your enemy would die. I have struggled with these feelings many times."

As his grandson listened at his knee, the old man continued, "It is as if there are two wolves inside me. One is good and does no harm. He lives in harmony with all around him and does not take offense when no offense is intended. He will fight only when it is right to do so and in the right way. But the other wolf? Ah! He is full of anger. The littlest thing will set him into a fit of temper. He fights everyone all the time for no reason. He cannot think because his anger and hate are so great.

"It is hard to live with these two wolves inside me, for both of them try to dominate my soul."

The boy looked intently into his grandfather's eyes and asked, "Which one wins, Grandfather?"

The old man solemnly said, "The one I feed, of course."

The Moral of the Story

Most of us struggle with the battle between good and bad that rages within us. Therefore always control your temper by deciding which wolf to feed.

THE BUS STATION

A company was hiring new staff for the post of risk assessment manager. One question on the written exam was the following:

> You are driving your car on a wild, stormy night. You pass a bus station, and you see three people waiting for the bus:
>   An old woman who looks as if she is about to die.
>   A doctor who once saved your life.
>   A man or woman you have been dreaming of as your spouse.
>
> You can take only one passenger in your car. Which one will you choose? Please explain your answer.

The candidate who was eventually hired out of two hundred applicants answered, "Give the car key to the doctor. Let him take the old lady to the hospital. I will stay and wait for the bus with the man or woman of my dreams."

The Moral of the Story

Life is like a bank account: you can't take anything out of it until you put something in. Sometimes we would gain more if we were able to give up our stubborn limitations and see life from a different perspective.

THE KING AND THE CONSULTANT

There once was a king who was fond of hunting. He was always accompanied by his consultant, who was very close to him. This consultant had a habit of saying to everyone, "Whatever happens, it happens for good."

During one of the king's hunting excursions, there was a terrible accident and his finger was chopped off. His consultant, per his habit, couldn't stop himself from saying, "Whatever happens, it happens for good." Since the king was the victim, he got very annoyed with the consultant and put him in jail.

On another hunting trip, the king was captured by cannibals and was about to be killed when they noticed his finger was missing. Per their tradition, they were not allowed to kill a person if any body part was missing. So they reluctantly set him free.

The king recalled the words of his consultant—"whatever happens, it happens for good"—and realized how true they were. He went to the consultant in jail and apologized for his mistake. However, the consultant said it was good that he was jailed. Otherwise he would have accompanied the king on the hunting trip and would have been eaten by cannibals.

Both men realized just how true the consultant's words were.

The Moral of the Story

Many times we are taken aback by the short-term impact of an event and don't realize how it is shaping our long-term future. It is nature's way of guiding our lives and making us realize that whatever happens, it happens for good.

Story #24

IN HOT WATER

Once upon a time, a daughter complained to her father that her life was miserable, and she didn't know how she was going to make it. It seemed like just as one problem was solved, another one followed.

Her father, a chef, took her straight into the kitchen, where he filled three pots with water and placed each on a high fire. Once the water boiled in all three, he placed potatoes in one pot, eggs in the second pot, and ground coffee beans in the third.

Then, without saying a word to his daughter, he let them boil. She moaned and waited impatiently, wondering what her father was doing. After twenty minutes he turned off all three burners. He then took the potatoes out of the pot and placed them in a bowl. He pulled the eggs out and placed them in a bowl. He ladled the coffee out and placed it in a cup.

Turning to his daughter, he asked, "Now, what do you see?"

"Potatoes, eggs, and coffee," she hastily replied.

"Look closer," he said, "and touch the potatoes."

She did and noted that they were soft. He then asked her to take an egg and break it. After pulling off the shell, she saw it had been hard boiled. Finally, he asked her to sip the coffee. Its rich aroma brought a smile to her face.

"Father, what does this mean?" she asked.

He explained that the potatoes, eggs, and coffee grounds had all faced the same adversity: boiling water.

"However," he noted, "each one reacted differently. The potato went in strong, hard, and unrelenting, but in boiling water it became soft and weak. The egg was fragile with a thin outer shell protecting its liquid interior until it was put in the boiling water. Then the inside of the egg became hard but easily broken. The ground coffee beans were unique. After they were exposed to the boiling water, they changed the water and created something new."

The Moral of the Story

In life things happen around us and to us, but the only thing that truly matters is what happens *within* us. Remember, everyone we know is facing, to some extent, his or her own private battles. Whether we succeed or fail depends on our reactions to stress. We can become soft like the potato and let the situation drive us; get rigid and more stubborn, as eggs do; or change the situation and create another environment altogether, as the coffee did. Regardless, the choice is up to us.

HEADS OR TAILS

During a momentous battle, a Japanese general decided to attack his enemy even though his army was greatly outnumbered. He was confident they would win, but his men were filled with doubt.

On the way to the battle, they stopped at a religious shrine. After praying with the men, the general took out a coin and said, "I shall now toss this coin. If it is heads, we shall win. If it is tails, we shall lose. Either way destiny will reveal itself."

He threw the coin into the air, and all watched intently as it landed. Lucky! It was heads. The soldiers were so overjoyed and filled with confidence, they vigorously attacked the enemy and were ultimately victorious.

After the battle a lieutenant remarked to the general, "It is destiny, and no one can change destiny."

"Quite right," the general replied as he showed the lieutenant the coin, which had heads on both sides!

The Moral of the Story

Life is all about attitude and perception. Therefore, if you look at the things around you in a positive way, you will attract positive results. It is not a secret or magic but the very rule of life. When you look at things in a positive manner, you are actually sending signals to your brain to deal with the situation with a positive approach. The result will be positive in much the same way sound repeated back becomes an echo. Try it for yourself: Yell a specific word, and the echo will reply back the same word many times.

AN EVEN PLAYING FIELD

Charles "Charley" Boswell (1916–1995) was blinded during World War II while rescuing his friend from a tank that was under fire. He had been a great athlete before his accident, and in a testimony to his talent and determination, after the war he decided to try a brand-new sport—one he'd never imagined playing even with his eyesight: golf!

Through determination and a deep love of the game, he became the US Blind Golf national champion thirteen times. One of his heroes was the great golfer Ben Hogan, so it truly was an honor for Charley to win the Ben Hogan award in 1958.

Upon meeting Ben Hogan, Charley was awestruck and stated that he had one wish in life, and that was to have one round of golf with the great Ben Hogan. Mr. Hogan agreed that playing a round together would be an honor for him as well, as he had heard about all of Charley's accomplishments and truly admired his skills.

"Would you like to play for money, Mr. Hogan?" Charley blurted out.

"I can't play you for money," said Mr. Hogan. "It wouldn't be fair."

"Aw, come on, Mr. Hogan," Charley persisted. "One thousand dollars per hole!"

"I can't. What would people think of me, taking advantage of you and your circumstance?"

"Chicken, Mr. Hogan?"

"OK," said a frustrated Hogan, "but I'm going to play my best!"

"I wouldn't expect anything else," said the confident Boswell.

"You're on, Mr. Boswell," said Hogan. "You name the time and the place."

A very self-assured Boswell responded, "Ten o'clock . . . tonight!"

The Moral of the Story

Never diminish your ability and let intimidation come between your reality and your potential. Get out of your shell and challenge the best in the industry. Remember, there are always ways to win. Even when you lose you will have learned from that experience— and you will have had the chance to learn from the best!

THE TURTLE

There once was a boy who found a turtle. He started to examine it, but the turtle pulled in its head and closed its shell like a vice. The boy was upset, and he picked up a stick to try to pry it open.

The boy's uncle saw all this and remarked, "No, that's not the way. In fact you may kill the turtle, but you'll still not get it to open up by using a stick."

The uncle took the turtle into the house and set it near the fireplace. It wasn't but a few minutes until it began to get warm. Then the turtle pushed out its head, stretched out its legs, and crawled.

"Turtles are like that," said the uncle, "and people too. You can't force them into anything. But if you first warm them up with some real kindness, more than likely they will do what you want them to do."

The Moral of the Story

People will resist you when they feel you are out for selfish goals and don't care about them. Just like a turtle, folks will close themselves off to you if you don't express a sincere interest in them first. Learn the art of warming up to people, and you will lead them toward your attention.

Story #28

YOU (ALMOST) SANK MY BATTLESHIP!

Two battleships assigned to a training squadron had been at sea on maneuvers for several days in heavy weather. The visibility was poor with patchy fog, so the captain remained on the bridge, keeping an eye on all activities.

Shortly after dark the lookout on the wing of the bridge reported, "Light, bearing on the starboard bow."

"Is it steady or moving astern?" the captain called out.

The lookout replied, "Steady, captain," which meant it was on a dangerous collision course with their ship.

The captain then shouted to the signalman, "Signal the ship: We are on a collision course. Advise you to change course twenty degrees."

A signal came back: "We advise *you* to change course twenty degrees!"

In reply the captain said, "Send: I'm a ship's captain. Change course twenty degrees now!"

"I'm a seaman second class," came the reply. "You had better change course twenty degrees now!"

By that time the captain was furious. He spit out a command: "Send: This is a battleship. Change your course immediately!"

The flashing light's reply: "This is a lighthouse!"

The battleship changed course.

The Moral of the Story

In life we face many obstacles and challenges that might push us to change our course of action. We should learn when to change our course to save energy, gain time, and secure harmony, within ourselves and the people with whom we interact. One of the most important traits of a good leader is learning the balance between authority and wisdom.

Story #29

THE BANK PRESIDENT

One day a new bank president met with his predecessor and said, "I would like to know what the keys to your success have been."

The older gentleman looked at him and replied, "Young man, I can sum it up in two words: good decisions."

To that the young man responded, "I thank you immensely for that advice, sir, but how does one come to know which are the good decisions?"

"One word, young man," replied the sage. "Experience."

"That's all well and good," said the younger, "but how does one get experience?"

"Two words," said the elder. "Bad decisions"

The Moral of the Story

Life is a learning journey, and there is no such thing as a good or bad decision, only a learning experience. Good decisions are almost always born from wrong decisions we made somewhere in our past and simply learned to avoid the next time.

Story #30

OUT OF SERVICE

An executive who suffered from poor self-esteem and a lack of self-confidence was promoted to a new position. Instead of facing the reality of his new job and working hard to overcome his weaknesses, he remained aloof and distant, with his door firmly closed to show how important and busy he was.

One day there was a knock at his door. He picked up the phone before inviting the visitor in. As the man waited to state his business, the executive kept talking on the phone, nodding and saying, "No problem, I can handle that." After few minutes, he hung up and asked the visitor what he could do for him.

The man replied, "Sir, I am from the IT department, and I am here to connect your phone."

The Moral of the Story

Hiding weaknesses by making yourself out to be a big deal, is just cheating yourself, not others; and if the people surrounding you are professionals, they can easily figure it out. Opening up and coming out of your shell is a better approach.

THE OBITUARY

Nearly a hundred years ago, a man looked at the morning newspaper and, to his surprise and horror, read his name in the obituary column. The newspaper had reported his death quite by mistake. His first response was shock.

Am I alive or dead? he wondered, peering more closely at the paper.

When he regained his composure, his second thought was to find out what people had said about him. The obituary's title read, "Dynamite King Dies." And in the text: "He was a merchant of death."

Turns out this man was the inventor of dynamite, and when he read the words "merchant of death" he asked himself a question: "Is this how I am going to be remembered?" He got in touch with his feelings and decided this was not, in fact, the legacy he wanted to leave behind.

From that day on, he started working toward peace. His name was Alfred Nobel, and he is remembered today for the great Nobel Prize named in his honor.

The Moral of the Story

Just as Alfred Nobel got in touch with his feelings and redefined his values, we should step back and do the same with our lives. What is the legacy we hope to leave behind? How would we like to be remembered? Once we answer these questions, we can more clearly determine if we are living up to the legacy we desire and, if not, redirect our course to take the proper journey.

Story #32

BIRD'S EYE

An ancient Indian sage was teaching his disciples the art of archery. He used a wooden bird as the target and asked them to aim at its eye. Before giving the first disciple a chance to try, the sage asked him to describe what he saw.

The disciple said, "I see the trees, the branches, the leaves, the sky, the bird, and its eye."

The sage politely asked this disciple to wait. Then he asked the second disciple the same question, and he replied, "I see only the eye of the bird."

The sage said, "Very good. Then shoot."

The arrow went straight and hit the eye of the bird.

The Moral of the Story

The art of achieving goals is ruled by three laws:

1. Focus on the target and concentrate by eliminating all the noise that may drag your attention from it.

2. Listen to your positive inner voice and learn from what you face within the journey.

3. Be honest with yourself; identify your gaps and work to close them by enhancing your ability.

Story #33

SOCRATES AND THE SECRET OF SUCCESS

One day a young man asked Socrates the secret of success. Socrates told the young man to meet him near the river the next morning to learn the answer. They met, and Socrates asked the young man to walk with him into the river. When the water got up to their necks, Socrates took the young man by surprise and swiftly dunked him below the surface.

The boy struggled to get out, but Socrates was strong and kept him there until the boy started turning blue. Socrates then pulled the young man's head out of the water. The first thing the young man did was gasp and take a deep breath.

Socrates asked him, "What did you want the most when you were there?"

The boy replied, "Air!"

Socrates said, "That is the secret of success. When you want success as badly as you wanted the air, then you will get it. There is no other secret."

The Moral of the Story

Just like anything else in life, success comes at a cost. We cannot get it until we pay the price in full. The price is an internal burning desire for achievement and focus on goals. In order to succeed, your desire for success should be greater than your fear of failure.

THE FROG AND THE PIT

A group of frogs was traveling through the woods when suddenly two of them fell into a deep pit. All the other frogs gathered around. When they saw how deep the pit was, they told the unfortunate frogs they would never get out. The two ignored the comments and tried to jump up out of the pit. The other frogs kept telling them to stop, that they were as good as dead.

Finally one of the frogs took heed of what the other frogs were saying and simply gave up. He fell down and died. The other frog, however, continued to jump as hard as he could. Once again the crowd of frogs yelled at him to stop the pain and suffering and just die. However, to the surprise of everyone, he jumped even harder and finally did get out.

One of the other frogs asked him, "Why did you continue jumping? Didn't you hear us?"

The group was shocked to discover that the frog was deaf, and all the time he had actually thought they were encouraging him to get out. He did not want to disappoint them and therefore did not give up.

The Moral of the Story

This story teaches two lessons: First, that our words contain the power of life and death. An encouraging word to someone who is down can lift him or her up and help him or her make it through the day. Second, a destructive word to someone who is down can be what it takes to kill him or her. Be careful of what you say; always speak life to those who cross your path.

The power of words is sometimes hard to understand. An encouraging word can go such a long way, yet anyone can speak words that rob another of the spirit to continue in difficult times. Special is the individual who will take the time to encourage another.

THE WOODCUTTER AND HIS AX

Once upon a time, a very strong woodcutter applied for a job with a timber merchant, and he got it. The pay was good, and so were the work conditions. For that reason the woodcutter was determined to do his best. His boss gave him an ax and showed him the area where he was supposed to work.

On the first day, the woodcutter felled eighteen trees.

"Congratulations," the boss said. "Go on that way!"

Very motivated by the boss's words, the woodcutter tried harder the next day, but he could bring down only fifteen trees. On the third day, he tried even harder, but he could bring down only ten trees. Day after day he was cutting down fewer and fewer trees.

I must be losing my strength, the woodcutter thought. He went to the boss and apologized, saying he could not understand what was going on.

"When was the last time you sharpened your ax?" the boss asked.

"Sharpen?" the woodcutter replied. "I've had no time to sharpen my ax. I've been too busy cutting down trees."

The Moral of the Story

Our lives sometimes get so hectic we do not take time to sharpen our axes to prepare for what comes next. In today's world, it seems, everyone is busier than ever, which leads to our forgetting to sharpen our skills, build up our abilities, and learn from the best. There is nothing wrong with activity and hard work. However, we should not get so preoccupied that we neglect to stay sharp and build our skills while on the working path.

Story #36

THE DISCIPLE AND HIS TEACHER

A disciple and his teacher were walking through the forest. The disciple was disturbed by the fact that his mind was in constant unrest. He asked his teacher, "Why are most people's minds restless, and only a few possess calm minds? What can one do to still the mind?"

The teacher looked at the disciple, smiled, and said, "I will tell you a story. An elephant was picking leaves from a tree. A small fly came buzzing by. The elephant waved it away with his long ears. Then the fly came again, and the elephant waved it away once more. This was repeated several times.

Then the elephant asked the fly, "Why are you so restless and noisy? Why can't you stay for a while in one place?"

The fly answered, "I am attracted to whatever I see, hear, or smell. My five senses pull me constantly in all directions, and I cannot resist them. What is your secret? How can you stay so calm and still?"

The elephant stopped eating and said, "My five senses do not rule my attention. Whatever I do, I get immersed in it. Now that I am eating, I am completely immersed in eating. In this way I can enjoy my food and chew it better. I rule and control my attention, not the other way around."

Upon hearing these words, the fly's eyes opened wide, and a smile appeared on his face. He looked at the elephant and said, "I understand! If my five senses are in control of my mind and attention, then my mind is in constant unrest. If I am in charge of my five senses and attention, then my mind becomes calm."

"Yes, that's right," answered the elephant. "The mind is restless and goes wherever the attention is. Control your attention, and you control your mind."

The Moral of the Story

Control your restless mind. Immerse yourself in whatever you are doing not only to enjoy it more but to do it better. In this way every endeavor becomes an opportunity to learn more about yourself and master the situation at hand.

THE GRADUATE

A recent graduate attended an interview for a customer service position at a major company. The post was attracting a lot of candidates, and the competition was intense.

The graduate did his best to answer the tricky questions, but when he finished the interview he left the room with little hope of being called back for the post. Feeling dejected, he walked away staring at the ground. In the corridor he picked up a piece of litter and threw it into a trash can. The interviewer passed by just then and saw it.

After two weeks the graduate got a call from the company, offering him the job.

The Moral of the Story

Remember that life is what happens when you think nobody is watching, so live with good habits, and you will be recognized! Doing more gains more, and doing less loses more.

THE WISE ADVISOR AND HIS STUDENTS

Many centuries ago a wise advisor welcomed his students to the last class on their educational path to becoming counselors to different governors in the large kingdom.

He took them to the fish pond on a farm, and he told one of them to throw a stone into the water. He asked them all to watch the circles the stone created. Then he asked each of them to think of themselves as that stone.

"You may create lots of splashes in your life," he said. "But the waves that come from those splashes will affect and disturb the peace of all your fellow creatures. Remember that you are responsible for what you put in your circle, and that circle will touch many other circles. You will need to live in a way that allows the good that comes from your circle to send the peace of that goodness to others. The splash that comes from anger, jealousy, or bad attitude will send those feelings to other circles. You are responsible for both."

The Moral of the Story

You are responsible for the lives of all you touch, however minor the relationships you might have with your fellow humans. Be wary of sending out negative ripples and always strive to be a positive influence on the lives of others.

THE ARK'S RULES

During the pearl era, a fisherman caught a talkative redfish that immediately began bargaining for her freedom.

"Hi there, nobleman," she said. "Let me go, and I will teach you eleven rules I learned from Noah's ark."

The fisherman considered the redfish's offer before deciding to let her go. As promised the redfish gave him the eleven rules of Noah's ark:

1. Don't miss the boat.

2. Remember we are all on the same boat!

3. Plan ahead. It wasn't raining when Noah built the ark.

4. Stay fit. When you're sixty years old, someone may ask you to do something really big.

5. Don't listen to critics; just get on with the job that needs to be done.

6. Build your future on high ground.

7. For safety's sake, travel in pairs.

8. Speed isn't always an advantage. The snails were brought onboard with the cheetahs.

9. When you're stressed, float a while.

10. Remember, the ark was built by amateurs, and the *Titanic* by professionals.

11. No matter the storm, there's always a rainbow waiting.

The Moral of the Story

We can all learn from these eleven rules that hearken back to simpler times. Remember that life can be simple if you allow it to be.

THE THREE STONECUTTERS

One day a traveler walking along a lane came across three stone-cutters working in a quarry. Each was busy cutting a block of stone. Interested to find out what they were working on, the traveler asked the first stonecutter what he was doing.

"I am cutting a stone!" he said.

Still no wiser, the traveler turned to the second stonecutter and asked him what he was doing.

"I am cutting this block of stone to make sure it's square and its dimensions are uniform," he answered, "so it will fit exactly in its place in a wall."

A bit closer to finding out what the stonecutters were working on but still unclear, the traveler turned to the third stonecutter. He seemed to be the happiest of the three, and when asked what he was doing he replied, "I am building a palace."

All three stonecutters were doing the same thing, but each gave a very different answer.

The Moral of the Story

Each of the three stonecutters knew how to do his job, but what set the third stonecutter apart? Perhaps it was these five distinguishing characteristics:

1. Knowing not just *how* and *what* to do, but *why* to do it.

2. Viewing the whole and not just its parts.

3. Seeing a vision—a sense of the bigger picture.

4. Having the ability to see significance in work beyond the obvious.

5. Understanding that a legacy will live on whether in the stone of a cathedral or in the impact made on other people.

THIS TOO SHALL PASS

A king called all of his wise men and counselors together for a meeting. He addressed them: "I want you to go and think, read, and research. Consult the wisest and most learned men in the land. Spare no expense. I want you to find the one statement that will get me through all situations in life whether I am on top of the world or in the pits. I don't want to learn long and complicated philosophies. I want one simple statement. Find it or write it—I don't care. Just bring me the statement."

The men left and looked for this statement for months. They finally returned and handed the king a scroll. He unrolled it. On it was written four words: "This too shall pass."

The wise men explained: When you are on top of the world, which is but a fleeting moment, things change; always remember that this too shall pass. When you are in the pits, all nights are followed by day; at your lowest moments also remember that this too shall pass. All external circumstances and material things change. No matter what your circumstances, remember, this too shall pass.

The Moral of the Story

All external circumstances and material things change. No matter what your circumstances, remember that they will not last forever. Everything changes at some point. All you have to do is wait.

THE LIONS AND THE GAZELLES

Lions love to eat gazelle meat. However, it is very difficult to catch gazelles because they run so fast. The older lions are too old and tired to be part of the chase; many are missing teeth and would never be able to catch their own meat.

Working together, the lions catch gazelles. Here's how.

The group of young lions chases the gazelles. The gazelles easily outrun the lions and head off in the direction the lions have chosen, which is, unbeknownst to the gazelles, toward a deep, grassy area where a group of older lions are hiding.

When the gazelles are driven within close range of the older lions, the lions jump up and roar loudly. Immediately the gazelles, responding to their perceived fear of imminent death, turn and run in the opposite direction—right into the mouths of the young lions.

The Moral of the Story

Running from our fears and not facing them can often lead us into real danger and even worse outcomes. Running away may mean we remain stuck and unhappy for a long time or until we face and move through our fears.

Story #43

EFFICIENCY VERSUS EFFECTIVENESS

It's said that Henry Ford once enlisted an efficiency expert to examine the operation of his company. While the expert's report was generally favorable, he did express reservations about a particular employee.

"It's that man down the corridor," he explained. "Every time I go by his office, he's just sitting there with his feet on his desk. He's wasting your money."

"That man," replied Ford, "once had an idea that saved us millions of dollars. At the time I believe his feet were planted right where they are now!"

The Moral of the Story

The importance of trusting people and nurturing their creativity can never be overestimated. We would all do well, therefore, to remember the difference between efficiency and effectiveness, and know which one we value the most.

Story #44

BACKSEAT DRIVERS

A husband was making fried eggs for breakfast one morning. Suddenly his wife burst into the kitchen.

"Careful," she said. "*Careful*! Put in some more butter. Oh my gosh. You're cooking too many at once. *Too many*! Turn them. *Turn them now*! We need more butter. Oh my gosh! *When* are we going to get *more butter*? The eggs are going to *stick*. Careful. *Careful*! I said be *careful*. You *never* listen to me when you're cooking. Never. Turn them! Hurry up. Are you *crazy*? Have you lost your mind? Don't forget to salt them. You know you always forget to salt them. Use the salt! *Use the salt. The salt*!"

The husband stared at her wide eyed and baffled. "What in the world is wrong with you?" he asked. "You think I don't know how to fry a couple of eggs?"

The wife calmly replied, "Of course, dear. I just wanted to show you what it feels like when I'm driving."

The Moral of the Story

When you are supervising or observing other people performing a task, be empathetic. Don't project your anxiety onto them and don't assume they are incompetent at what they're doing. No one performs well with another person hovering over them, giving instructions. Let the other people do their jobs, and give them the same right to make the mistakes that you give to yourself.

THE FARMER AND THE PROFESSORS

A group of learned professors chose to take a relaxing vacation at a remote farm, far from the madding crowd of the city where they lived. Their host was a simple farmer who had never seen the inside of a school.

The professors were astonished to see the order and discipline with which the farm functioned. Corn and wheat grew aplenty in the fields, the orchard yielded delicious fruits, and healthy cows and calves gazed peacefully on the green meadows. The little farm prospered beautifully.

"How did you manage all this?" one of the professors asked the humble farmer.

"I am afraid I am uneducated," he replied. "So I use only my brain."

The Moral of the Story

The secret to management is very simple: Apply common sense quite commonly.

THE MILLION-DOLLAR LESSON

Tom Watson Jr., who was CEO of IBM between 1956 and 1971, was a key figure in the information revolution. Watson repeatedly demonstrated his abilities as a leader, never more so than in the following story.

A young executive had made some bad decisions that cost the company several million dollars. Watson summoned him to his office.

The young man fully expected to be dismissed. As he entered the office, he said, "I suppose after that set of mistakes, you will want to fire me."

Watson is said to have replied, "Not at all, young man. On the contrary, we've just spent a couple of million dollars educating you."

The Moral of the Story

Always strive to see the big picture. An ordinary manager would have fired the young executive—and the company would have lost his costly experience. In a mistake there can be great value, if only we choose to recognize it.

NOT ENOUGH CHICKENS

A butcher who had had a particularly good day proudly put his last chicken on a scale and weighed it. "That will be six dollars and fifty cents," he told the customer.

"That's a good price, but it really is a little too small," said the woman. "Don't you have anything larger?"

Thinking fast, the clerk took the chicken to the refrigerator, paused, and then returned to the counter with the same chicken. "This one," he said, "will be seven dollars."

The woman paused and then made her decision. "I know," she said. "I'll take both of them!"

The Moral of the Story

Whatever our daily goals might be, we should remain honest and ethical in doing business and dealing with unexpected circumstances. We should also be cautious in evaluating our acts and decisions and their impact on our business relationships.

THE SLEEPING FARMHAND

A young man applied for a job as a farmhand. When the farmer asked for his qualifications, he said, "I can sleep when the wind blows." This puzzled the farmer. But he liked the young man and hired him anyway.

A few days later, the farmer and his wife were awakened in the night by a violent storm. They quickly checked things out to see if all was secure. They found that the shutters of the farmhouse had been tightly fastened. A good supply of logs had been set next to the fireplace. The young man slept soundly.

The farmer and his wife then inspected their property. They found that the farm tools had been placed in the storage shed, safe from the elements. The tractor had been moved into the garage. The barn was properly locked. Even the animals were calm. All was well.

The farmer then understood the meaning of the young man's words—"I can sleep when the wind blows."

Because the farmhand did his work loyally and faithfully when the skies were clear, when the storm broke he was prepared. When the wind blew, he was not afraid. He could sleep in peace.

The Moral of the Story

In this life, do your part perfectly in a manner that satisfies you and leave the rest to destiny. If you prepare for rain when the skies are clear, you too will sleep soundly when the wind blows!

Story #49

THE CEO AND THE BANANA

John DeLorean told one of his close friends that shortly after he had become general manager of Chevrolet, he attended a sales conference in Dallas. When he arrived at his hotel suite he discovered that someone from the company had delivered a huge basket of fruit to his room. While talking to an associate about the basket's size and variety, he said that when he'd first seen the assortment he had thought, "What? No bananas?"

From that moment on, the word throughout General Motors was "John DeLorean loves bananas." No matter how many times he attempted to explain that he had only meant to be amusing, bananas kept showing up in cars, chartered planes, hotel suites, and in meetings, and followed him throughout his career at Chevrolet.

The Moral of the Story

Be careful what you say when you are leading a team. On many occasions subordinates will consider the words of their leader as directions even though they are not. Most of us live with preconceived perceptions, but don't forget: A false perception is the mother of mistakes.

Story #50

THE SALESMEN

Many years ago a British shoe manufacturer sent two salesmen to a remote area of Africa to investigate and report back on market potential.

The first salesman reported, "There is no potential here—nobody wears shoes."

The second salesman reported, "There is massive potential here—nobody wears shoes."

The Moral of the Story

The two salesmen used exactly the same words—"nobody wears shoes"—to describe the situation. Yet one of them saw this as negative and a disadvantageous situation, while the other saw it as positive and a good opportunity that needed to be captured. Be careful about how you view the world, and remember to try to see opportunities even in the most seemingly negative situations.

THE SURGEON AND THE MECHANIC

A heart surgeon took his car to his local garage for routine maintenance service. As usual, he exchanged a little friendly banter with the owner, a skilled, but not especially wealthy mechanic.

"So tell me," said the mechanic. "I've been wondering about what we both do for a living and how much more than me you get paid."

"Yes?" said the surgeon.

"Well, look at this," said the mechanic, indicating a big, complicated engine on which he was working. "I open it up, check how it's running, fix the valves, and put it all back together so it works as good as new. We basically do the same job, don't we? Yet you are paid ten times what I am. How do you explain that?"

The surgeon thought for a moment, smiled gently, and replied, "Now try it with the engine running."

The Moral of the Story

Look beyond the task someone is completing and dig deeper. People are recognized and rewarded not based on hard work alone but on challenges, risk mitigation, and task sophistication, and on how all of those are handled.

THE PRICE OF EXPECTATIONS

"Tell me about the people at the organization you just left," said a senior manager who was actively screening candidates to fill a key leadership role.

"They were uneducated and lazy," the candidate responded. "I always had to keep an eye on them because they were constantly trying to goof off or defraud the company. They were lousy communicators, resisted change, and cared only about themselves."

"That's too bad," replied the senior manager. "I'm sorry to say that's the same type of people you'll find here. This doesn't sound like a job you would enjoy."

To the next candidate the manager asked the same question.

"Oh, they were great," she said. "Although many of them couldn't read, and we had some trouble communicating with each other, they were very driven to succeed. Once we all got to know each other, they were constantly helping one another and working together."

"Great," the senior manager responded. "That's the same type of people you'll find here."

The Moral of the Story

Remember that people live up to—or down to—a leader's expectations. Expect more, and you will get more. Expect less, and you'll get just that.

THE DURIAN TREE

An eighty-year-old man was planting a durian tree. (A durian is a thorny fruit with a very pungent smell. It is known as the "king of fruits" and is very popular in Southeast Asia.)

A neighbor observed this and asked the old man, "Do you expect to eat durian from that tree? After all, it will take eight to ten years to bear fruit."

The old man leaned on the handle of his spade and smiled. He said, "No. At my age I know I won't. All my life I have been enjoying durians, but never from a tree I have planted. If other men had not done what I am doing now, I would never have had durians. I'm just trying to repay the other men who planted durians for me."

The Moral of the Story

Life is like a bank account: You will never be able to withdraw from it if you do not put some savings into it first. Therefore a person should be *giver* first and *taker* second in everything he or she does. Eat from the durian trees of your ancestors, but be sure to plant a few before you're gone as well!

THE VIOLIN LESSON

One day a music teacher was listening to one of his students play. When the student was done, his teacher said, "Stop playing the violin for one week. There is something else you must learn. Live by looking for things to do for other people. For example, pick up your friend's books when they have fallen. This is your homework for the week."

The astonished student asked, "What does doing things for other people have to do with violin practice?"

"When listening to your performance," the teacher said, "I could clearly feel that you were self-centered in your heart. If your heart is set to work for others, your mind will be able to work more sensitively in an expanded world. More abundant, delicately beautiful expressions will enter your performance."

The Moral of the Story

Great talent and a deep, beautiful feeling in the heart are tied closely together. Doing things for others increases our empathy, and increased empathy helps us lead others more emphatically. Not unlike violin playing, management is an art that becomes higher as human values become more highly developed.

Story #55

THE TEACUP

A great Japanese master received a university professor who had come to inquire about wisdom. The master served tea. He poured his visitor a full cup and then kept on pouring. The professor watched the cup overflow until he could no longer restrain himself.

"Stop!" he cried, yanking the cup away. "Can't you see that it's full? No more will go in."

"Like this cup," the master said, "you are full of your own opinions and speculations. How can I show you wisdom unless you first empty your cup?"

The Moral of the Story

Knowledge is understanding based on experience, while wisdom is the spirit behind applying the knowledge. To receive knowledge, wisdom, and best practices, you first have to empty your thoughts of opinions, prejudgment, and speculation.

THE HAIRCUT

A wise, old barber welcomed a young, new client into his chair. "What are we doing to your hair today?" asked the barber.

The client shrugged, buried his head in a sports magazine, and said, "Surprise me."

The barber smiled to himself and eagerly set to work. When he was through with his latest masterpiece, he tapped his client on the shoulder and said, "What do you think?"

The client looked up and was surprised by his own reflection. The barber had given him a military-style flat top that didn't match his client's business attire whatsoever.

"What have you done?" asked the client, leaping out of the chair with alarm.

The barber replied, bemused, "I surprised you!"

The Moral of the Story

It's easy to fall into a rut, particularly with life's day-to-day routines. However, no event—not even a simple haircut—is ever unimportant. Don't waste today staring down at your shoes until bedtime. Look up, look around, be involved, be alert, and, above all, be interested in the proceedings of your life.

THE LITTLEST WAVE

This story is about a little wave bobbing along in the ocean, having a grand old time. He was enjoying the wind and the fresh air until he noticed the other waves in front of him crashing against the shore.

"My God," the wave exclaimed. "This is terrible. Look what's going to happen to me!"

Then along came another wave. It saw the first wave looking grim and it said to him, "Why do you look so sad?"

The first wave said, "You don't understand—we are all going to crash! All of us waves are going to be nothing. Isn't it terrible?"

The second wave said, "No, you don't understand. You're not a wave. You're part of the vast and powerful ocean."

The Moral of the Story

Alone we are just drops of water; together we are an entire ocean. The value of a person is not based on individual performance but on how he or she contributes to the team, society, and even the entire universe.

Story #58

THE FLY AND THE ANT

One day the fly said to the ant, "I am better than you."

The ant smirked and said, "*I* am better than *you*."

"How so?" buzzed the fly, landing on a nearby leaf.

"I am stronger than I look," said the ant. "I can carry many multiples more than I weigh, and I am low to the ground."

"I can fly," said the fly.

"But you're alone," said the ant.

"But I can fly."

"So can I," said the ant, and with that a million of his friends poured from the mound and lifted him high, high, high into the air, each clinging to the next as they built a mountain where once there had been just one ant.

The fly buzzed, ever out of reach, ever triumphant. "That's not flying," he said, buzzing away, ever alone.

The ant looked back at his friends gathered together, smiling in unison. "Tell *them* that," he said.

The Moral of the Story

Don't make the mistake of comparing yourself to others, particularly when envy is the only payoff. Instead spend more time looking inward, at yourself, to find the strengths that make you soar.

THE DETOUR

A man got lost while driving through the countryside. As he tried to reach for a map, he accidentally drove off the road and into a ditch. Though he was not injured, his car was stuck deep in the mud. He walked to a nearby farm to ask for help.

"Warwick can get you out of that ditch," said the farmer, pointing to an old mule standing in a field. The man looked at the decrepit beast and then back at the farmer, who just stood there repeating, "Yep, old Warwick can do the job."

The man figured he had nothing to lose. The two men and the mule made their way back to the ditch. The farmer hitched the mule to the car. With a snap of the reins, he shouted, "Pull, Fred! Pull, Jack! Pull, Ted! Pull, Warwick!"

And the mule pulled that car right out of the ditch.

The man was amazed. He thanked the farmer, patted the mule, and asked, "Why did you call out all of those names before you called Warwick?"

The farmer grinned and said, "Old Warwick is just about blind. As long as he believes he's part of a team, he doesn't mind pulling."

The Moral of the Story

The spirit of teamwork has a magical effect that can be summarized in the following five ways:

1. It creates an effective working mood among all team members.

2. It creates a highly productive atmosphere.

3. It helps sustain high performance and synergy among the team members.

4. It creates a consciousness among the team members, which leads them to focus on results and achievement.

5. Never underestimate the power of collaboration!

Story #60

THE WARRIOR

A great warrior stood beside a battlefield, preparing for war. He was so calm and poised that a nervous foot soldier just had to ask, "Great warrior, we are largely outnumbered and certainly out-gunned. How can you stand there so confident and self-assured?"

"It's simple," he told the foot soldier. "I always go into battle prepared to die. That way I have nothing to lose and, hence, nothing to fear."

The Moral of the Story

We cling too tightly to what we possess and not tightly enough to what is possible. Fear the man with nothing to lose, for he is a great power unto himself—and others.

THE VIOLINIST

One cold January morning, a man stood in a crowded Metro station in Washington, DC, and started to play a Bach piece on a violin. Since it was rush hour, thousands of people went through the station while he played, most of them on their way to work.

As the minutes went by, no one stopped. Then a middle-aged man slowed his pace and stopped for a few seconds before hurrying to catch his train.

A minute later the violinist received his first dollar tip—from a woman who threw the money in his till and, without stopping, continued to walk.

A few minutes later, someone leaned against the wall to listen to him, but then looked at his watch and started to walk again. Clearly he was late for work.

In the forty-five minutes the musician played, only six people stopped to listen. Twenty gave him money but continued to walk at their normal paces. He collected a total of thirty-two dollars. When he finished playing and packed up his violin, no one noticed. No one applauded, nor was there any recognition.

The hurrying commuters didn't recognize him, but the violinist that morning was none other than Joshua Bell, one of the best concert violinists in the world. At the subway station he had played one of the most intricate pieces ever written, using his Stradivarius violin worth $3.5 million dollars.

The Moral of the Story

In many situations we come across very special people. However, we pass up the opportunity to enjoy being with them, to learn from them, or to give them the recognition they deserve for a simple reason: our own ignorance. How much better would our lives be if we quit making assumptions and started making contact?

Story #62

THE EXAM

Two freshman roommates had an exam on the last day of the semester. The first freshman did as he always did; he went about his routine, slept normal hours, and remained calm. The second freshman tried to cram everything he'd forgotten all semester long into hours-long late-night study sessions, fueling himself with caffeine pills and plenty of coffee.

As the two walked into the exam room, one calm and the other frazzled, the second freshman asked his roommate, "How do you do it? You haven't studied for this test all week."

"I don't calling it studying," said the first freshman. "I call it learning, and I do it every day."

The Moral of the Story

Learning is not an event, but a habit. Those who practice it every day rarely need to study, while those who rarely practice it find that no matter how much they study, it's never quite enough.

Story #63

THE VACUUM SALESMAN

A new vacuum cleaner sales rep knocked on the door of the first house on a street. A tall lady answered. Before she could speak, the enthusiastic sales representative barged into the living room, opened a big black plastic bag, and poured salt onto the carpet.

"Madam," exclaimed the eager sales representative. "If I cannot clean this up with the use of this new powerful vacuum cleaner, I will *eat* all this salt!"

"Would you prefer chili sauce or ketchup with that?" asked the lady.

The bewildered sales representative asked, "Why, madam?"

"Because there's no electricity in the house."

The Moral of the Story

Don't make assumptions! Before jumping into work on a new project and committing yourself, be sure you are aware of the entire situation and circumstances surrounding that project. Convincing others can never be done by forceful assertion alone. It has to be according to a systematic approach that takes into account the different factors related to the situation.

Story #64

THE PEDICURE

A woman sat in a salon chair, getting a pedicure. She looked around the busy salon, anxiously glancing from patron to patron.

"Looking for someone?" asked the nail tech at her feet.

"My friend," said the woman. "I thought I saw her black Mercedes parked out front, but I don't see her."

"The Mercedes? That's mine," replied the salon tech.

"Yeah, right," huffed the woman, still looking for her friend. "How could you afford a Mercedes?"

The salon tech paused from massaging the woman's ankles and said, "I work ten hours a day, six days a week, and I've been here for five years. I live simply, have no credit cards, and own my home. I have a waiting list of regular clients who all tip me exceedingly well because I'm professional, dependable, and loyal. That's how I—"

The pretentious woman interrupted her. She demanded to see a manager and asked to be served by a different tech.

The nail tech didn't mind; she had a line of customers waiting to fill the canceled appointment.

The Moral of the Story

Never judge a book by its cover or a person by his or her position. Everyone has to start somewhere—even the world's richest billionaires. Someone who dresses very modestly may be a billionaire, while someone who flaunts his or her wealth may be bankrupt.

THE KING AND THE WISE MAN

One day a king said to his wise man: "When it comes to managing the monarchy, I consider myself more knowledgeable than you. However, I do admit that you are wiser. I would like you to simplify for me the difference between knowledge and wisdom."

The wise man answered the king as follows: "*Knowledge* is knowing that a tomato is a fruit, not a vegetable. *Wisdom* is knowing not to include it in a fruit salad."

The Moral of the Story

Wisdom is the ability to utilize your knowledge in the right situation at the right time with the right approach and steps, and with the right amount of excitement! Beware of people who can spout endless facts but don't know how to place them in context.

THE HOLIDAY

Snow was falling, and lights were blinking as the repairman arrived at a house on Christmas Eve. An irate young woman opened the door and addressed him with a vengeance.

"I can't believe this is happening tonight of all nights!" she barked as the young repairman walked inside, toolbox in hand. "I'm missing all my favorite holiday movies."

"I'm very sorry for the inconvenience," said the repairman. He found the TV and quickly got to work.

The customer paced anxiously until, several minutes later, he solved the problem—with a pair of AAA batteries.

"Your remote wasn't working," he explained.

"Finally," she huffed, snatching it from his hand and using it to make sure her television worked. "Now I can get back to my holiday routine."

The repairman met her eyes and said pointedly, "Me too."

The Moral of the Story

Everyone's time is equally valuable. Remember that if you feel put out over something inconvenient, chances are several other people are being affected by its ripple effect as well. Before you push the panic button or call for help, try to solve a problem yourself, or at least call during business hours!

And when you get the help you need, a simple "thank you" goes a long way.

THE ARTISTS

Dante Gabriel Rossetti, a famous nineteenth-century poet and artist, was once approached by an elderly man who wanted Rossetti to look at some sketches and drawings he had and tell him if they were any good or if they at least showed potential talent.

Rossetti looked them over carefully. After the first few, he knew they were worthless, showing not the least sign of artistic talent. But he was kind, so he told the elderly man this news as gently as possible. He was sorry, but he could not lie to the man.

The visitor was disappointed but seemed to expect Rossetti's judgment. He then apologized for taking up Rossetti's time, but would he just look at a few more drawings, these done by a young art student? Rossetti looked at the second batch of sketches and immediately became enthusiastic over the talent they revealed.

"These," he said. "Oh, these are good. This young student has great talent. He should be given every help and encouragement in his career as an artist. He has a great future if he will work hard and stick to it."

Rossetti could see that the old fellow was deeply moved. "Who is this fine young artist?" he asked. "Your son?"

"No," said the old man sadly. "I drew these, forty years ago. If only I had heard your praise then! For you see, I got discouraged and gave up too soon."

The Moral of the Story

If you really love to do something, keep at it! And always give your best to others who are striving to better themselves; never discourage them. There is no competition in helping others succeed, only the promise of adding more joy and talent to the world.

THE INTERVIEW

A job applicant sat across the desk from his potential manager, fidgeting in his seat. The manager considered his résumé with an impassive look before glancing at the applicant.

"What is your biggest strength?" the manager asked.

The applicant sagged a little; he'd been afraid someone might ask him this question. Unsure of how to answer, he said, "Knowing my weaknesses."

The manager frowned. "Which are?"

When the applicant was done listing his faults, the manager nodded and filed his résumé away. "I'm sorry, but we won't be making you an offer today."

The applicant nodded as if resigned to the fact. As he stood to go, the manager said, "If I may, a bit of advice: when I saw your résumé I was very impressed. You have a lot of skill, but it doesn't come across in person. I was disappointed that you didn't offer a better strength, only weakness."

The applicant then asked, "What would have been a proper answer to that question?"

The manager smiled. "Anything. It's not *what* the applicant answers that I pay attention to as much as *how* he gets excited about telling me what he can do well."

The Moral of the Story

Know your worth so that others may too. It is not prideful to make the most of your accomplishments, skills, or talents; rather, it is your mission in life to serve the world and those who employ you.

THE BUS STOP

A busy executive stood at a bus stop, late for work. Next to him a homeless man sat on the bus stop bench, holding a hat with which he collected donations from passersby. As the executive paced, anxiety building with each passing moment, he fretted over the meeting he was late for, who was there, and what they might think of him.

Traffic whizzed by on the busy city street, but there was not a bus in sight. Stepping off the curb to hail a cab, the executive heard shouting behind him and paused—just in time to narrowly avoid being hit by a delivery van.

Heart pounding, instantly soaked in sweat, the executive turned to find the homeless man smiling at him.

"Th-th-thank you," the executive spluttered, wide-eyed. "I didn't even think you'd seen me standing here."

"It was you who ignored me," said the homeless man. "But I never miss an opportunity to help someone in need."

The Moral of the Story

We can all help each other in some way. Mentors come in all shapes and sizes. Overlook appearances to get to know them better and seek the wisdom they have gained through their own life experiences, however humble.

THE ROCK FORMATION

One by one tourists waited to pose with a beautiful, timeless rock formation.

Nearby, another rock that had recently fallen close to the formation's side marveled at the popularity of this uniquely shaped stone.

"How can I become so beautiful?" asked the fallen rock.

"Stay right where you are," said the rock formation. "Enjoy the gentle drumming of frequent rains, the harsh freeze of ice, and the coat of frost. Enjoy the moss that grows along you and the dirt that rests beneath you, and in a few centuries' time you too will be a piece of art people will want to take pictures with."

The fallen rock scoffed. "I don't have time for all that. What can I do to become beautiful in a week or less?"

The rock formation scoffed too. "Find yourself a sculptor."

The Moral of the Story

Patience is not only a virtue but a benefit to those seeking success. When we are seasoned by time and wise from our years, we learn that not everything has to happen on our timeline; sometimes things really do happen for a reason.

Story #71

THE SALESMEN

Three car salesmen stood around the lot, spying potential customers.

Said the young, eager salesman to the senior salesman, "Let's run around and see who can sell the most cars to the most customers."

Said the second young salesman to the senior salesman, "Let's conquer and divide. You take the twelve on the left, and I'll take the twelve on the right."

Their senior salesman smiled and said, "How about I sell the nicest car to one customer and let his friends come to me after he brags about my one-on-one service?"

The Moral of the Story

People respond to sincerity and personal attention—and they can't wait to tell their friends about their good experience. Enthusiasm is important, but so are wisdom, patience, and pacing. To gather everything all at once is often less realistic and advantageous than simply taking your time and mastering the acquisition of all.

THE ART COLLECTION

An old man who had become estranged from his family left his vast art collection to his three children. One child was greedy, one was ambitious, and one was gentle.

Upon being shown into their father's mansion for the first time in decades, the children eagerly raced through the great halls, inspecting the colorful artwork hanging on the walls.

"I'm going to take my share and sell it to the highest bidder," said the greedy child.

"I'm going to take my share, open a gallery, and become a famous art dealer," said the ambitious child.

"I don't think you'll have much luck," said the gentle child.

"Why?" asked her siblings.

"Look closely," the gentle child said. "These aren't works of art. They're the art projects we made in school when we were growing up!"

The Moral of the Story

Knowledge, art, and beauty are to be shared, not hoarded and kept stockpiled in the attic. Share all that you possess, for only in sharing are our many gifts put to best use.

Story #73

THE PRAYER

A soldier stopped to pray before his first battle: "Dear Lord, please grant me the strength to overcome my aggressors, defeat my enemy, and return to my country in one piece."

His sergeant, hearing the boy's prayer, muttered one of his own: "Dear Lord, please grant this boy's prayer, for I'll be standing right next to him!"

The Moral of the Story

We rely upon each other for safety and success. Do your very best in every situation, because you'll not only be helping yourself but you'll also be helping those who depend upon you.

THE PSYCHIATRIST

A man went to his psychiatrist with a confession.

"Doctor," he said, "I'm a Peeping Tom. I can't help looking in people's windows."

The psychiatrist shook his head and offered the following advice: "You've been late on your last three bills. Since you'll never be able to cure your obsession, why don't you at least open up a window-cleaning service so you can make a decent wage at it?"

The Moral of the Story

We are all imperfect creatures. We all need to make the very best of the skills that we have—as long as what we do is moral and ethical! And if you have an illness—mental or physical—get the treatment you need.

THE MUSICIAN AND THE MAID

A talented musician was composing his latest masterpiece when the cleaning woman came in.

"What do you think?" he asked, proud of his new work.

"Beautiful," she said, running her hands along his grand piano. "Just beautiful! This will hardly need any dusting this week at all."

The Moral of the Story

Beauty is in the eye of the beholder. Talent and art can be very subjective. We all come to situations with our own baggage and take from them what we want to. Don't be discouraged when your intentions are lost on others. Instead learn to appreciate others' tastes and welcome input from a variety of sources.

THE SPORTS CAR AND THE JALOPY

While mired in traffic, two cars remained side by side for nearly an hour. One was a sleek and gleaming red sports car, polished bright and shiny. The other was a wheezing jalopy covered in rust spots.

Since the jalopy had no air conditioning, its owner had the windows down. At one point the sports car's owner rolled down his window, took off his sunglasses, and said, "Nice car. Where'd you get it, the junkyard?"

The jalopy's owner shrugged and said, "Your car may be faster, but all that horsepower won't get you out of this traffic jam any sooner than my jalopy."

The Moral of the Story

Pride goeth before a fall and oftentimes robs us of perspective. Is a sleek car worth the price tag or is it better to drive a car we've paid off and use the money we saved for wiser investments? And remember—an expensive sports car won't get you to your destination any faster than a modest sedan.

TWO FORTUNE COOKIES

Two men were sitting in a Chinese restaurant when the bill came. They cracked open their fortune cookies. The first man chuckled and crumpled his fortune into a ball while the second man gasped.

"What's wrong?" asked the first man.

"Wrong?" answered the second man. "Nothing's wrong. Everything's right. Look at my fortune!" He held it out. It said, "Great things will happen to you today." The first man laughed.

"What's so funny?" asked the second man.

"Mine said the same exact thing," said the first man.

"Then what are we waiting for?" said the second man, dragging his partner out of his seat. "Let's go make great things happen!"

The Moral of the Story

Ideas come from the strangest places, especially when you're not looking for them. Create a habit of allowing for inspiration at any time of the day or night and in any place, not just when you have time for it.

THE TIP

A new waiter approached one of his colleagues, beaming.

"What's up?" asked the old waiter.

"That guy just left me a hundred dollars as a tip!" exclaimed the new waiter.

Curious, the old waiter looked up just in time to find the customer leaving the restaurant. "That's Bill," he explained to the newbie. "He comes in once a week."

"Why is he so generous?" asked the new waiter.

The old waiter smiled. "He bussed tables here while he was going to college. He told us all that if he ever made it big, he would come back and leave big tips every time he ate here."

"So he's a millionaire now?"

"Hardly," said the old waiter. "He's the manager at the department store across the street."

"That's making it big?" asked the new waiter.

"It is to a busboy!"

The Moral of the Story

Success means something different to everyone. Follow your own compass, and let it guide you to where you want to go, not to where you think all the other successful people are headed.

TWO GARDENS

Two women—one old, one young—lived next door to each other. Each tended her own garden.

The young woman worked tirelessly to protect her garden from pests, erecting elaborate traps, consulting local pest-control companies, and constantly spraying pesticides. Her garden flourished, but it was a full-time job.

The old woman worked tirelessly as well but on her own. When rabbits and field mice raided her garden, she didn't chase them away but instead sat on a bench and chatted pleasantly with them.

"How can you abide those pests eating all your vegetables?" asked the young woman one day, peering over the fence that separated their yards.

"They're not pests," said the old woman. "They're friends. Who else would share all my beautiful vegetables with me?"

The Moral of the Story

Life is based on perspective. When we are young, we tend to see most things as threats. As we age we tend to welcome challenges and turn them into opportunities.

Story #80

THE HUMMINGBIRD AND THE SNAIL

A hummingbird hovered above a snail, marveling at its slow, lethargic pace.

"Aren't you frustrated by going so slow?" asked the hummingbird.

"No," said the snail.

"Look at how fast I can fly," said the hummingbird, flitting here and there. "Bet you've never moved even half this fast in your entire life, have you?"

"No," said the snail. "But I'll live twice as long as you, so I figure I have that much more time to get where I'm going."

The Moral of the Story

Prioritize what is important to you and live with a sense of calm, quiet contentedness. Just because there is a rat race doesn't mean you have to join it.

THE CONFESSION

A parishioner stepped into the confessional and prepared to bare his soul. "Forgive me, Father," he said, kneeling and gesticulating as he'd been taught years earlier, "For I have sinned."

"Ain't we all?" asked the voice on the other side.

The parishioner, confused, muttered, "Yes, well...I had racy thoughts on Thursday and cursed on Wednesday."

"You call those sins?" asked the voice. It was unfamiliar to the parishioner, but he assumed it was just another visiting priest.

"Sure—don't you?" asked the parishioner.

"Not hardly," said the voice.

"W-w-well," the parishioner stammered. "How should I proceed?"

"I think you should quit sweating the small stuff, pal," said the voice. "Because life is short, and you're doing OK so far in my book."

"What kind of priest are you?" blurted the parishioner.

"I'm not the priest," said the voice on the other side of the screen. "I'm the janitor."

The Moral of the Story

Confession may be good for the soul, but living right helps you avoid having to confess in the first place. None of us is perfect, but we can strive to live by a code of a virtuous life whether or not anyone else is looking.

THE PAINTING

A haughty woman stood admiring a piece of art at the local art gallery.

"It's so ironic," she said to the stranger standing next to her. "So retro kitsch."

"Really?" asked the stranger.

"Oh yes," she said. "Look at the bold colors. Look at the simplicity of its lines. See the way it uses text combined with a rectilinear industrial frame to create visual tension. And its placement on the wall is brilliant—it forces you to consider your position within the space of the room. It makes you choose whether to stay or go."

"What would you expect to pay for a work such as this?" the stranger asked.

The woman turned to him, curling up her nose at his ignorance. "For a piece such as this? Easily six figures."

"Well, it's not for sale," said the stranger. "It's the 'exit' sign."

The Moral of the Story

False modesty and pride are two of life's most unattractive traits. Never try to bluff your way out of a situation or pretend to be someone you're not. Ignorance is not stupidity but merely a lack of information—and it's easily rectified.

THE CASHIER

It had been a long day by the time the customer arrived at the checkout stand. The cashier greeted him with a smile, rang up his order, and bagged it quickly.

The customer was amazed; he'd never seen such efficient service from a minimum-wage worker.

"I know we're all busy," he said, "but is there a manager I might speak to? Or the owner?"

The cashier blushed, nodded, and said, "I'm the owner. Is something wrong?"

The customer was impressed and said so. "Quite the opposite. In fact I was going to tell the owner how great a cashier you are."

"You still can," she said.

"But why are you bagging my order today?"

"Two of my employees called in sick at the last minute," she explained, "and I didn't want to close the store early. So I decided to put on my apron and get back to work."

"I must say," said the customer, gathering his bags. "I've never had an owner give such good service before."

"I may be the owner today," she said, flashing that same sincere smile. "But I started as a cashier, and I can't forget how that felt."

The Moral of the Story

Humble beginnings are life's way of teaching us our most valuable lessons. Never deny where you've come from or what lowly positions you may have worked. Instead allow them to inform your future with humility, respect, and courtesy.

THE PEBBLE, THE ROCK, AND THE BOULDER

A pebble was rolling downhill, enjoying his day, when he got stuck next to a large rock.

"If you could just move," said the pebble, "I could get on my way."

"That's what I said two hundred years ago," grumbled the rock.

"What's stopping you?" asked the pebble, eager to get on with his day.

"Ask him!" the rock said with a chuckle, shrugging toward the giant boulder he was wedged against.

"Why can't *you* move?" said the pebble to the big boulder.

"Settle in, kid," said the boulder to the pebble. "Until this mountain I'm wedged against moves, none of us is going anywhere."

The Moral of the Story

We never know where we're going to end up, so it's best to avoid making enemies of the people with whom we might be spending a large amount of time. It pays to try to get along with everyone.

TWO SQUIRRELS

Two squirrels hustled about, gathering nuts for the winter. The first squirrel carefully secreted away twice as many nuts as the second.

As the fall days dwindled and winter approached, nuts became harder and harder to find. Soon it was snowy and cold, and the squirrels could eat only what they had stored away.

One day the second squirrel said to the first, "All my nuts are gone. I fear I won't have enough for the winter."

"You said that last winter," said the first squirrel. "And the winter before that."

"Yet every year you manage to share your nuts with me," recalled the second squirrel fondly.

"Why do you think I squirrel away twice as many nuts as I can eat every year?"

The Moral of the Story

Preparation is the foundation of many a success story, but so is charity. Those who think of others tend to succeed more often because they can sympathize not just with their charities but with their customers as well.

Story #86

THE LEAF AND THE BRANCH

A great tree towered over the forest floor. At the very top, the smallest branches could each support only a single leaf.

One day a leaf said to its branch, "I'm going to take my chances on the breeze. I'm leaving you today."

"But why?" asked the branch.

"Because I'm tired of spending all my time in this tree," said the leaf. "I want to explore the world."

"But then you'd be gone, and I'd have no one to talk to all day."

"What about all these other branches?"

"They all have leaves to talk to," said the branch. "Why don't you wait until fall? Then the other leaves will all be gone, and the other branches will talk to me again."

"I can't wait that long!" said the leaf. "You'll just have to get along without me."

The leaf shrugged, wriggled, and—pop!—fell from the branch, leaving it far, far behind. Bolstered by the wind, the leaf flew far, far away. It traveled here and there, seeing road and barns and streets and people, until the breeze stopped, and the leaf fell to the ground far, far from home.

Night came and with it darkness, and the little leaf trembled all alone. It had enjoyed its journey, but now it had neither the other leaves nor its branch to talk to. It withered, cold and alone, until it shriveled up and died.

The Moral of the Story

It is important to travel and explore, but to do so alone ignores the power of friendship to color, inform, and add to our lives. And when you do travel, make sure you have a way to get back home.

THE KEY

A homeowner was taking out his trash when he saw an old woman trying to unlock his neighbor's door.

"Can I help you?" asked the homeowner.

"Oh no," said the woman, wriggling a key around in the lock. "This isn't the house."

"Isn't *what* house?" asked the homeowner.

"The one that goes with this key," said the old woman.

Intrigued, the homeowner asked, "What key?"

The old woman was only too happy to tell her. "Years ago," she said, "I found this key at the bus stop. I've been trying it out on houses ever since."

"But it could take years before you find the right house," said the homeowner. "Decades even. Why bother?"

"Simple," said the old woman. "Imagine how happy the homeowner will be to get his key back!"

The Moral of the Story

Don't be in such a hurry to solve every mystery. Let life unfold before you, and play the cards you are dealt without worrying what is in the rest of the deck. Focusing on what you don't have will always ensure that you neglect what you do have. And be sure to tackle only those projects that are worth the effort and sacrifice.

THE APPLE, THE BANANA, AND THE NUT

The apple said to the banana, "My skin is red and tangy. People love its crunchy texture."

The banana said to the apple, "My skin is yellow and protects me. People have to peel it to get to my sweet flesh."

The nut said to them both, "My skin is ugly, hard, and tough to crack. People need a metal tool just to get a taste of what's inside me, which isn't very sweet."

The banana asked, "Then why bother?"

"Because getting there," said the nut, "is half the fun."

The Moral of the Story

Sometimes the journey is just as much fun as the destination. And when the task is challenging, the reward can seem that much better.

THE FOXHOLE

While bleeding to death from their wounds, two soldiers climbed into a foxhole to spend their last few moments on Earth.

"I can't believe I'm going to die so young," said the first soldier.

"I can't believe I made it this long!" said the second.

The Moral of the Story

Perspective is a powerful thing. How we perceive the world determines how much—or how little—we value our time on this planet.

Tomorrow is never promised to us; and to assume otherwise is to invite folly into our lives. Live each day as your last, and always be amazed, refreshed, renewed, and inspired when you rise to live another one.

Story #90

THE INTERPRETER

A manager returned to the factory floor after attending a weekend seminar. He walked around nodding to his many workers. The production line was a melting pot of races and nationalities, many of whom spoke Spanish. Since the manager didn't, he had to trust his interpreter.

At the end of a very long day, the manager turned to his interpreter and said, "You're fired."

"What? Why?" asked the interpreter.

"Because all day long, you've been telling me production is up when it's down. That profits are down when they're up. If I can't trust you, I can't keep you on anymore."

"But I spoke only Spanish. There's no way you could know all that," said the interpreter, realization spreading across his face. "Wait...what class did you take over the weekend?"

The manager answered, "How to Learn Spanish in a Weekend!"

The Moral of the Story

Be careful about what you say. You never know who's listening—or how much they understand. The truth is universal and can be understood in any language.

THE UNEMPLOYED

Made redundant at his job, a young man was suddenly let go. Unable to find work in his field, he was forced to survive on meager unemployment checks.

Day after day, as his savings dwindled, the young man tried to make the best of his situation. When the bank repossessed his car and he had to take the bus, he thought, *Great. I'll meet lots of new people.*

When he could no longer afford the bus, he thought, *Great. Now I'll walk everywhere and get in really good shape.*

When he began losing weight and couldn't fit into half his clothes, he gave them away and thought, *Great. Look at all this new closet space I have.*

When he had to move out of his expensive apartment into a cheaper, smaller one, he thought, *Glad I got rid of all those extra clothes!*

When the young man finally found a steady job, he was a new man. He took nothing for granted, never wasted a moment or a cent, and quickly rose through the ranks. When he was honored at his retirement many years later, someone asked him about the best day of his life.

"When I got fired," he said.

"Why?" someone asked.

"Because that was the day I learned that the only thing I could really count on was myself."

The Moral of the Story

From adversity can come a new beginning. There is power in perspective. Those who make the best of things often lead better lives when it counts the most.

THE RACCOON AND THE CAT

One day a raccoon watched from the bushes as a kind old lady fed a stray cat. When the raccoon ventured forth for his own free meal, the woman screamed and swatted at him with her broom.

After the old lady had gone inside the house, the raccoon asked the cat, "How come she feeds you and not me?"

The cat smiled and purred, "Because people like cats and hate raccoons."

The next night when the old lady returned, the raccoon was ready. The cat eagerly lined up for his food, but the raccoon stayed put.

"Meow," said the raccoon from his hiding place.

The woman promptly slid a dish of food into the bushes.

The Moral of the Story

Prejudice and prejudgment can hold us back from achieving great things—if we let them. Improvising, adapting, and overcoming let us write our own success stories regardless of how others try to edit them.

Story #93

THE DUEL

Two great gunfighters squared off in the middle of town.

"When I say 'draw,'" said the referee, "walk ten paces, turn, and fire."

The gunfighters nodded, and the referee said, "Draw!"

The first gunfighter turned and walked away. The second gunfighter stood right where he was, lifted his gun, and hit the first in the back, killing him.

"Why did you do that?" asked the referee, who was red in the face. "Now you'll be branded a coward and a scoundrel for the rest of your life."

The second gunfighter shrugged, holstering his weapon. "At least I'll *have* a life," said the coward and scoundrel, smiling as he walked into the nearest saloon.

The Moral of the Story

When choosing between popularity and survival, survival usually wins. Sometimes survival means making difficult and even dangerous choices.

THE RECEIPT

A customer glanced at his receipt before putting his bags back in his cart. He noticed a surcharge for the store's plastic bags.

"What's this extra fee?" he asked the cashier.

"We now charge you one cent per bag," she replied. "If you bring in your own bags, we won't charge you."

"Thank you," said the customer. Then he left the store.

Weeks later the customer returned bearing a handful of recyclable bags. As the cashier loaded up his groceries, she said, "These bags are great! Where did they come from?"

"Your competitor," said the customer. "I came in here only because they were too crowded."

The Moral of the Story

Be careful not to cut off your nose to spite your face. In other words, provide quality service or goods at a fair price, and don't try to nickel and dime your loyal customers until they finally get fed up and go elsewhere.

THE MOSQUITO AND THE BEE

A mosquito flitted from arm to arm, drinking his fill of human blood.

A bee went from flower to flower, soaking up pollen for his hive.

"You have that great stinger," said the mosquito. "Why don't you ever use it?"

"I can use it only once," said the bee, "so I'm very careful about where I stick it."

"I stick mine anywhere," said the mosquito. "I don't have to be careful."

"Then how do you know what your worth is?" asked the bee before buzzing away.

The Moral of the Story

Know what's so important to you that you'd die for it and what's only important enough to live for. Life is a marathon, not a sprint, and those who cross the finish line too soon often find themselves at odds with how to live the rest of their lives.

THE OBITUARY

A wife sat down to write her husband's obituary. After pondering the opening line for hours, she finally smiled and wrote the following: "My husband, Bill, was the funniest man I ever met. Unfortunately his best lines were reserved for his eight mistresses. While they might have been entertained by him, they won't be getting a dime of his estate!"

The Moral of the Story

The mistresses may have had fun with Bill while he was alive, but they were short-term relationships. It was the wife, to whom he was legally married, who would inherit his wealth.

In death we are often revered even if we don't deserve it. Our goal should be to live a life worthy of reverence, especially from those who know us the best.

THE SNAKE IN THE GRASS

A snake slithered into the grass.

A gardener squealed and cried, "Eek! Snake!"

"Relax," said the snake. "I'm not going to hurt you, so why are you screaming?"

"I'm not scared of you," said the gardener. "I'm calling my six pit bulls over to tear you to pieces!"

The Moral of the Story

No matter how strong we think we are, there is always someone stronger. Resist the temptation to play the bully, boss, or villain; after all, the hero has a much longer life expectancy.

THE NURSE AND HER PATIENT

A nurse was struggling with the worst. Patient. Ever.

He was old, rude, cantankerous, and crusty.

"Get this!" he bellowed, waving his cane. "Get that!" he cried, pushing the "call" button.

Finally the nurse had had enough. "Why are you being so rude and obnoxious?" she asked.

The old man smiled. "You remind me of my wife," he chuckled. "I'm just making myself feel at home."

The Moral of the Story

We never know what baggage other people bring from their lives into ours. Knowing is half the battle; knowing how to deal with them is the other half.

THE SINGER

A famous singer, known for being a diva, walked onstage.

"Good evening, ladies and gentleman," she said. "I've just been informed that my band can't make it, so I'm going to sing my entire set *a cappella*. I hope you don't mind."

For two hours straight, the singer tore the roof down with blistering renditions of all her hits, sung completely without accompaniment.

Later, when a fan asked her why she had done it, her answer was simple: "I may have a bad reputation, but I've been allowed to have a bad reputation because I'm a great singer. Tonight I bought myself a free pass to act as badly as I want to for as long as I want to."

The Moral of the Story

We tend to accept bad behavior from the most talented people despite the fact that we wouldn't tolerate it from anyone else. Don't fall into the trap of behaving worse with each new success; instead use each success as an excuse to behave more successfully.

Story #100

THE RED CARPET

An old woman hired a laborer to finish her walkway with red carpet. Once the job was done, the laborer asked the old woman why she had made such an unusual choice for her walkway.

"I wanted to be an actress my whole life," she told the laborer. "Instead, I worked as a librarian. Now that I'm old and retired, I know I'll never be able to walk the red carpet at a big movie premier, but now I can walk it on the way into my house every day!"

The Moral of the Story

Never give up on your dreams. Even if they don't come true as expected, make them happen some other way. Adapt, overcome, turn left instead of right, do whatever you must to live the life you always wanted to—even if it isn't exactly how you thought it might turn out.

THE HOARDER

One day an old man's grandchildren came to help him clean out his attic. His grandson stumbled across an old trunk. He opened it and found it stuffed to the gills with old movie-ticket stubs.

"Grandpa!" said the grandson. "You're a hoarder. What are you doing with all these ticket stubs?"

The old man smiled and said, "Those are the tickets from every movie I ever saw with your grandmother. From our first date, to the first year we were married, and then until the week she died, we went to two movies a week. Some men collect love letters; I collected movie tickets."

The Moral of the Story

Memories are powerful things; to deny them is to deny a big part of life. Embracing the future is an important part of success, but so is celebrating—even cherishing—the past.

Story #102

THE RUNNER AND THE WALKER

A walker enjoyed his morning constitutional every day, spending a solid hour looping around his favorite track. Most mornings a runner passed him time after time. But every few days, the walker noticed, the runner would skip his morning rounds.

One day it happened that the walker and the runner finished their morning routines at the same time. As they stretched on the sidelines the runner said, "Why do you walk when running is so much better for you?"

Instead of answering, the walker asked, "Where do you go when you're not here?"

The runner shrugged. "Sometimes I pull or strain a muscle. It takes a few days for me to recover."

The walker nodded. "I walk every morning and never pull or strain anything. I enjoy it, and I feel perfectly healthy, without injury or pain. Now, who's to say which is better for me?"

The Moral of the Story

March, walk, or run to your own drummer. Don't let those who think they know best sway your decisions. After all no one knows you better—or is more interested in seeing you succeed—than you.

THE NOVELIST

A young woman moved in downstairs from an old man. Every afternoon, just before teatime, the woman could hear the man typing in the apartment above hers.

It went on for weeks, and then months—but only for a few minutes a day.

One day the young woman was out in the lobby getting the mail at the same time as the old man.

"Excuse me," she finally worked up the courage to ask, "May I inquire as to what you're writing every afternoon?"

The old man blushed and said, "I'm working on my novel."

"Congratulations!" said the young woman. "When will it be done?"

"Oh my," said the old man. "At this pace, not for another ten or twenty years."

"Why is it taking so long?" asked the young woman.

"Well, you see, I love to write," explained the old man, "but only in short doses. So I write for fifteen minutes every afternoon just before teatime."

"Don't you ever want to write more?" asked the young woman. "Or faster?"

The old man shrugged and said, "Not really. I figure every word I write brings me closer to my goal. What's the rush?"

The Moral of the Story

Everybody goes at their own pace. We often compare ourselves to others and find fault in how they operate. Be confident in your skills and enjoy your progress so you don't grow frustrated with the skills or progress of those you lead.

THE JANITOR

A janitor worked at a school for forty years. When he retired he asked if he could attend the students' graduation ceremony that year. He was surprised when, upon learning he would be in attendance, the student body asked if he could hand out the diplomas—a task generally performed by the school's principal.

As the graduation ceremony dragged on, the janitor handed out all the diplomas except for one. When he opened it up, he found his own name printed on it. When the janitor told the principal he didn't deserve it, the principal quickly corrected him: "You spent forty years performing the same job. That took stamina. You spent forty years dealing with spoiled brats. That takes patience. You spent forty years cleaning bathrooms. That takes humility. If anything you deserve a doctorate, not just a high school diploma."

The Moral of the Story

Beware those who do not respect people who earn less than they do. Humility is an essential part of human nature, and those who don't have it—or can't appreciate it—are clearly damaged goods.

THE DOCTOR AND HIS PATIENT

A patient went to see his doctor.

"Doctor," said the patient. "My head hurts, and my legs are restless. What should I do?"

"Walk home from my office," said the doctor. "The walk will cure your restlessness and likely cure your headache as well."

The next day the patient showed up beaming. "Great news, doctor," he said. "I took your advice and walked home from your office yesterday. My legs feel great, and my headache is gone."

"I've got good news too," said the doctor. "Your car was towed, so if you walk to the gas station where they towed it, you should feel even better."

The Moral of the Story

See the upside of bad news. Negativity will never be in short supply, but if you choose to think about it differently, you can take away most of its power to derail your day.

THE CHEF AND THE CHILD

A great chef had prepared a feast for a royal family. As a liveried butler served the meal, the king boasted, "Truly, this is the finest roast pork I've ever had."

The queen raved, "The braised venison is to die for!"

The princess squealed, "You have given new life to this goose."

The prince, however, was not impressed. At seven years of age, he was interested only in dessert; yet he saw nothing in the cakes and puddings and fancy pastries that had been loaded onto the table.

"Isn't there any chocolate?" he asked.

The chef turned up his nose and said not a word, but a fast-thinking butler slid a hand into his pocket and pulled out a cheap candy bar he'd been saving for later.

"Here you go, prince," said the butler, and the boy pronounced the dime-store milk chocolate the best he'd ever had.

While the chef was incensed and stormed from the room, the king and queen were relieved and made the butler their personal servant.

The Moral of the Story

Never let pride get in the way of progress. Pleasing your toughest critic will always make pleasing your biggest fans just that much easier!

THE LION TAMER

For years the lion tamer cracked his whip, and for years his lion bowed and scraped. One day the tamer forgot his whip and stepped into the cage with his lion anyway.

"We have known each other for years," said the lion tamer. "I no longer need a whip to master you."

The lion growled, roared, and promptly ripped the tamer in two.

"Why are you doing this?" asked the lion tamer with his dying breath.

"Because I am a lion," said the wild beast, "and you never asked if I wanted to be tamed. If you had, I would have told you that I didn't."

The Moral of the Story

Don't assume that those we lead want the same things as we do. We must work as a team to achieve specific goals but not always in the same way. Be conscious of the needs of your teammates, and in return they will respect your sense of empathy.

THE SNOW AND THE RAIN

The snow fell, and people cheered. The rain fell, and people frowned.

One day the rain asked the snow, "Why do they like you and hate me?"

"Because snow is pretty and rain is ugly," said the snow, falling to great applause.

Then the rain smiled as he fell and fell, turning the snow hard and slick and dangerous.

"How do you feel about ice?" the rain laughed.

The Moral of the Story

In life, your situation can change overnight. What was popular yesterday may be unpopular tomorrow; humility can help you enjoy success while it lasts and prepare for failure before it comes.

Story #109

THE USHER

A moviegoer waited in line to get into the latest summer blockbuster. He noticed that after tearing each ticket, the usher would smile and politely say, "Thank you for silencing your cell phone."

When it was the moviegoer's turn, the usher tore his ticket, smiled, and said, "Thank you for silencing your cell phone."

"Why do you say it like that?" asked the moviegoer.

"Well, sir," said the usher, "We've found that five times out of ten, if we ask customers to turn off their cell phones nicely, they do it. When we demand it, nine times out of ten they don't. At least this way, we're getting a better return on our investment."

The Moral of the Story

You may catch more flies with honey than with vinegar, but you'll never know until you try both.

THE MONK AND THE TOURIST

A monk sat in his garden, observing nature. A tourist wandered over and sat next to him.

"I know you can't talk," said the tourist, "but I just want to tell you how beautiful your garden is."

"Thank you," said the monk.

The tourist gasped. "I thought you'd taken a vow of silence."

"No," said the monk, smiling. "Just a vow to speak only when necessary."

The Moral of the Story

Silence may indeed be golden, but you wouldn't know it to hear people talk. Learn to listen more so that when you do talk, you know just what to say.

CONCLUSION

Have you been inspired by this book? Edified? Enlightened? And hopefully entertained? Then my work here is done— but yours is just beginning. Please continue to share these stories with those you love, respect, admire, work with, play with, learn with, or simply think might need them.

Wisdom is best when it is shared. In sharing we all grow wiser with each new story, tale, allegory, or fable. I am collecting new stories all the time and look forward to the moment when I can share another one hundred and ten of them with you.

Until then, be safe, be kind, be thoughtful, and be wise. We owe ourselves and others at least that much. You can continue sharing your short stories and the morals on sharoqalmalki@gmail.com

Made in the USA
Middletown, DE
15 November 2016